1892

John Abbott resigns; John Thompson becomes prime minister.

Gilbert Parker publishes *Pierre and His People*.

Edmonton incorporated as a town; population 700.

Pauline Johnson begins public readings of her poetry.

A Novel and Unique Entertainment

A RECITAL

BY

Miss E. Pauline Johnson

Of Brantford (the well-known Indian poetess)

Of her own stirring and strong compositions, including "The Avenger," "A Cry from an Indian Wife," "As Redmen Die," and "The Song my Paddle Sings," assisted by Mrs. Maggie Barr Fenwick, soprano; Mr. Fred Warrington, baritone; Mr. W. S. Jones, organist, in

ASSOCIATION HALL, FRIDAY EV'NG, FEB. 19

Tickets 25 and 50c. Plan opens Tuesday, February 16, Nordheimer's.

Actress Marie Dressler (Leila Koerber) of Cobourg, Ont., makes first appearance on Broadway.

James A. Naismith of Edmonton, Alta., develops game of basketball in Springfield, Mass.

The First Basketball Team

Composing room workers strike Toronto's *Evening News* and launch the *Star*.

THE HAMILTON MFG. CO.

Lead, zinc and silver deposits discovered at Kimberley, B.C.

Fire devastates downtown St. John's, Nfld; 10,000 homeless.

Royal commission appointed to consider national prohibition.

The biggest cheese in the world (13 tons) made at the Dominion Experimental Dairy Station at Perth, Ontario.

Louis Fréchette publishes *Originaux et détraqués*.

First automatic telephone switchboard introduced.

1893

The Earl of Aberdeen appointed governor general.

Bliss Carman publishes *Low Tide on Grand Pré,* his first volume.

Frederick Featherstonhaugh of Mimico, Ont., builds Canada's first electric car.

Toronto's Jake Gaudaur wins world's sculling championship in Austin, Texas.

Earthquake registers heavy shocks in Montreal.

Dr. Wilfred Grenfell establishes Labrador Medical Mission for deep-sea fishermen.

Vancouver Civic Museum and City Art Gallery established.

Calgary, Alberta, incorporated as a city; population 4,000.

National Council of Women of Canada founded by Lady Aberdeen.

THE NATIONAL Council of WOMEN

Edited by THE COUNTESS OF ABERDEEN

NOTES OF THE COUNCIL.

Fire destroys year-old Robert Simpson Co. building in Toronto.

A Woman's Store

"*The hand that rocks the cradle rules the world.*"

THE old saying expresses a truth which may be applied to the business world even more directly. Woman rules everywhere throughout civilization directly or indirectly, and nowhere are her wants, wishes and whims catered to more devotedly than in this big store. It is emphatically a woman's store, like it should be, since women have the most buying and providing to do, and the Richmond Street wing, where men's clothing is sold, is called The Mens' Store, to distinguish it for that very reason. The store as a whole is a Woman's store.

THE ROBERT **SIMPSON** COMPANY LIMITED **Toronto, Ont.**

1894

...nders ...est-seller,

...eal Amateur Athletic Assoc. defeats Ottawa, 3-1, in first Stanley Cup game; attendance: 5,000.

Toronto's Athaeneum Club wins the first Dunlop Trophy bicycle race in Toronto.

John Thompson dies; Mackenzie Bowell becomes prime minister.

Joseph Pope publishes *Memoirs of the Right Honourable Sir John Macdonald*.

Bank failures lead Newfoundland to propose union with Canada.

Labor Day celebrated for first time in Canada.

Amelia Yeomans founds Manitoba Equal Franchise Club for women's rights.

The Naughty Nineties

Above: *Toronto "newsies" hustle a top-hatted business executive at Queen and Yonge in 1894. Bicycles and electric streetcars splash past the rush-hour crowd.*

Previous page: *Minstrel shows were all the rage in the nineties, and, although few Blacks lived in Canada, this plantation orchestra and chorus won acclaim.*

June Callwood
The Naughty Nineties
1890/1900

Canada's Illustrated Heritage

Canada's Illustrated Heritage

Publisher: Jack McClelland
Editorial Consultant: Pierre Berton
Historical Consultant: Michael Bliss
Editor-in-Chief: Toivo Kiil
Associate Editors: Michael Clugston
　　　　　　　Clare McKeon
　　　　　　　Harold Quinn
　　　　　　　Jean Stinson
Assistant Editor: Marta Howard
Design: William Hindle
　　　　Lynn Campbell
　　　　Neil Cochrane
Cover Artist: Alan Daniel
Picture Research: Lembi Buchanan
　　　　　　　Michel Doyon
　　　　　　　Betty Gibson
　　　　　　　Christine Jensen
　　　　　　　Laurie McElhinney
　　　　　　　Margot Sainsbury

ISBN: 0-9196-4421-X

N.S.L. Natural Science of Canada Limited
254 Bartley Drive
Toronto, Ontario M4A 1G1

Printed and bound in Canada

This nineties' pin-up showcard must have shocked quite a few strait-laced Victorians. Despite the décolletage of the young lady's dress, high "choker" necklines dominated respectable fashion throughout the decade. However, the hair style here is strictly the period vogue, made popular by American illustrator, Charles Dana Gibson.

Contents

PROLOGUE   *Twilight of a Century* 6

ONE   *New Money* 12

TWO   *Living Recklessly* 24

THREE   *Hard Times* 36

FOUR   *Two Solitudes* 48

FIVE   *The Railway Comes to Come-By-Chance* 58

SIX   *Penny-Farthings, Boneshakers and Silver-Singers* 68

SEVEN   *"Those New Women"* 80

EIGHT   *The West to the Rescue* 92

NINE   *The Licence to Practise* 106

TEN   *Lady Aberdeen's Diary* 118

Acknowledgements 124

Index 125

Picture Credits 128

Twilight of a Century

The day is coming when this country will have to take its place among the nations of the earth. . . .

Wilfrid Laurier, June 1890

The nineties witnessed the sunset of the Victorian ethic, the passing of a time when the role and importance of God, the Queen, the flag, duty, honour, virtue and family life were all clearly defined. It was the twilight of an age, the end of a century, when one good opinion, on any topic, could last a lifetime; when there was right and wrong without shades in between; when there was no confusion about what to believe and what to trust. Faith in the church, the British Empire and hard work gave shape and stability to life.

The "Britishness" of Canada rose to a crescendo with the celebration of Queen Victoria's Diamond Jubilee in 1897. But as the country's and the century's last great expression of loyalty and devotion to the crown subsided, something new emerged, something that would grow stronger as the country—lusty, confident, ambitious—swung into the next century. The people were beginning to feel, well, *Canadian*.

The old order was passing. The decade would witness great technological developments that would start moving the coal and wood stoves out of the kitchen, advance the science of medicine, bring recorded music into the home, and put the country first on two, then comfortably on four wheels. The voice of women would be heard. Things were not going to be the same again.

There was strength and stamina in the nineties but it was not a tranquil decade. It was marked by a depression, one of the worst the young country had known, and torrid summers that baked crops to dust. In the newly industrialized cities, children worked sixty-hour weeks, bloody strikes and lockouts greeted labour's growing voice as ragged workers threw bricks and were clubbed in turn by the militia.

Stores, farms and homes stood vacant as half a million Canadians left the country to find work in the States. One in every ten citizens departed, exceeding by half again the trickle of immigrants.

Yukon gold strikes in the last half of the nineties helped to get the economy moving, slowly, and good harvests on the Prairies helped the CPR pay its way. Towards the end of the decade the mood of the country became joyful, enthusiastic and confident, almost obscuring the dark resentments lingering in Quebec. The hanging of Riel a decade earlier left a mistrust of Confederation, aggravated by a bungled and drawn-out affair history calls the Manitoba school question.

During a bitter six-year fight over French-language Catholic schools, a federal government was defeated and Quebec saw itself as a beleaguered island. The province sent agents scurrying into the

The Rose Bud *repertoire included "The Flying Trapeze," "Love at First Sight," and 68 other hits.*

Opposite page: *Queen Victoria's 1897 Diamond Jubilee was the occasion for public and private celebration. This Acadian couple toasts with ice cream while uncle sticks to the hard-stuff. Among flags, portraits and lanterns, the focus of interest is a modern new gadget: the cylinder phonograph.*

mill towns of New England states, trying to persuade French-Canadians to return home to bolster defences, but few were attracted.

Meanwhile, to fill the still vacant Prairies a campaign was launched to recruit immigrants. Europe's farm belts were flooded with posters and pamphlets extolling the fertility of the prairie soil and the cheapness of the land. The good land in the United States was already homesteaded, but Canada still had to attract farmers and peasants fleeing taxes and military drafts.

death in the autumn

As the economy revived, stores and factories were opening again, which meant that dirt streets could be paved, wooden bridges could be replaced with iron ones and a start could be made on improved sewage disposal in order to reduce typhoid deaths, a regular feature of the Canadian autumn.

An indigenous Canadian middle class had formed. It bore no resemblance to the urbane, anti-monarchist, sophisticated aristocracy of Europe. Canada's leading social class was emerging from shopkeepers and bankers and bore the stamp of stiff, duty-conscious prudery. They were nervous about their new prestige and jealously guarded its borders.

An organized women's movement rallied around the prohibition issue. It was their perception, not far off the mark, that the country was drinking itself to death. Visitors from other lands formed the impression that the country was populated almost entirely by drunks. Whisky and beer were cheap and plentiful. Catalogues advertised medicine that would put colour into the cheeks — little wonder as it was half alcohol. Champagne was administered to passengers on trains to ward off motion sickness and whisky to hospital patients about to undergo surgery.

By the end of the decade, Canadians were cele-

brating a new-found affluence following a lengthy depression. Nothing was too much. Ornamentation was impressed on everything, from cornices to cupboards. Tables tottered under dense arrangements of bric-a-brac, windows were smothered in layers of curtains and fringed drapes, women's hats drooped under a weight of birds, silk roses, plumes and veiling. The affluent indulged in prodigious amounts of food, twelve courses at a single meal, and admired what they called "a fleshy look," indeed, a mark of prosperity. Life for the poor was much the same as ever. The new century would not change it.

The well-to-do lived in huge, daffy houses that bubbled with turrets and rang with the sounds of as many children as the women could bear. Housemaids, or domestics, looked after the business of cooking, cleaning, washing, polishing and answering the door.

But toward the end of the nineties there was no excess to compare with the country's adoration of the bicycle. The country went "bicycle mad," and a few fanatics believed the vehicle would change civilization.

free and easy

In fact, it did. Bicycle prices were high in terms of nineties' incomes, but almost everyone managed to acquire one, somehow. Electric street railways had already broadened horizons and enabled people to live some distance from the factories; but the bicycle provided a much greater freedom. Clerks and gentry pedalled side by side, sharing the open road, tales of adventures and their patching kits. Some saw this free and easy manner as a dangerous dissolving of the social order. The contraption had the unforeseen consequence of loosening the grip churches exerted over social and intellectual life as the bicycle, unlike the streetcar, ran on Sundays. Clergymen thundered against the

As shopping by catalogue gained in popularity, and competition from big-city department stores became almost tooth-and-nail, small-town general stores like Frieze & Roy of Maitland, N.S., took to ads on shopping bags to sell a medley of dry goods and housewares.

godlessness of the bicycle, to no avail.

The vehicle had a profound effect on women. To begin with, it released them from waist-pinching corsets which Paris vogue decreed must be tighter each season. For the first time in memory, the female ankle was exposed – gaitered of course – and, even more shocking, some women wore a voluminous sort of pant called bloomers.

There was an innocent charm about the nineties. In Vienna, Sigmund Freud was about to introduce a universe of fixations, phobias, complexes and sexual frustrations. However, few Canadians believed that people were more complicated than they seemed. Marriage was for life, only scoundrels went to jail and the poor were lazy, obviously. Attaining "Entrance," the Grade 8 final examination, was all the education the average man needed.

Men were not devious. If they disliked one another, they said so. Public men accused one another of corruption, drunkenness and stupidity – publicly of course. Newspaper invective was fulsome. Audiences that disapproved of a speaker would make such an uproar that no voice from the podium could be heard and if sufficiently exercised, they occasionally climaxed the evening by breaking all the movable furniture in the hall.

The Victorian ethic posed little threat to bullish private enterprise. The doctrine of social welfare was just beginning to show in the Protestant conscience, although the "poor box" had always been a fixture of Roman Catholic churches. There was little general concern about the brutality of prisons and the starvation and filth in the slums, but concern, whether sincere or affected, was growing.

It was an era of great contrasts, of chastity and brothels, censorship and pornography. It was a decade of crippling poverty and bounteous windfall; tough bosses and violent labour disputes; an age of cesspools and sterilization, plagues and dramatic medical advances; French-English conflict; prairie droughts and booms; gold rushes and emigration; puritanical men and militant women; sporting heroes and Klondike hurdy-gurdy girls. It was the Naughty Nineties.

"Wages of Sin," the greatest of all melodramas, was not only praised by the press but endorsed by the clergy. Fifty cents bought the best seat in the house at the Toronto Opera.

In the nineties' bicycle boom, Canadian enthusiasts kept up-to-date with Cycling – *"A Mirror of Wheeling Events."*

Main Street, 1890

Main Street, Canada, in the 1890s reflected the hustle and bustle of a growing nation. Victoria and Vancouver on the Pacific were thriving, attracting trainloads of new citizens. Prairie towns were extending their city-limits almost each year despite the hard times in the middle of the decade.

In the East cities were becoming sophisticated metropolises with paved streets, electric arc lights replacing older gas fixtures, and large stone office buildings crowding small two- and three-storey houses. As the decade wore on, horse-drawn carriages surrendered the right-of-way to new electric street railways and bicycles, and by the end of the century, the newest new-fangled vehicle, the motor car, made its debut.

Kingston's Princess Street in 1890 was pretty much in stride with cities of its size. By the turn-of-the-century this thoroughfare would be neatly paved.

Edmonton's dapper gentlemen line muddy Jasper Avenue in 1899. Between 1891 and 1901, the city's population grew by leaps and bounds from 700 to 2,626.

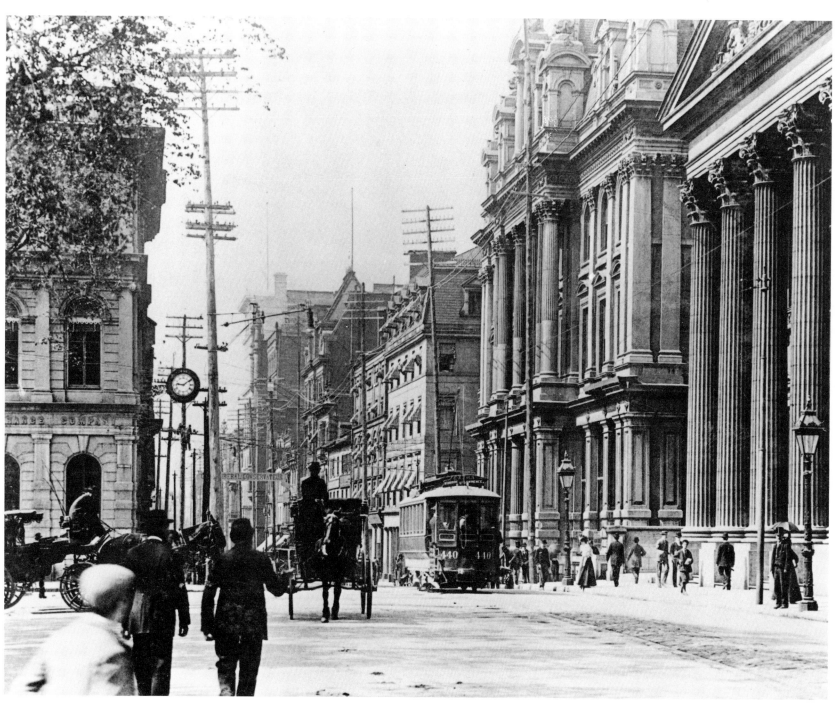

Montreal's temples of finance changed the look of St. James Street at Place d'Armes. It's 1896, and by the clock (it's 9:10 A.M.), some of these office workers are late.

CHAPTER ONE

New Money

*In the cities we have the rich and poor,
the classes and the masses, with all that these
distinctions involve. . . .*

J. S. Woodsworth

It was the best of times to become rich. Tariffs and grants could be manipulated, towns were crazy for railways, labour was cheap and humble, dazzling technological discoveries created a mass hunger for acquisition, and incomes were tax-free.

The mid-nineties depression lifted to reveal a country infatuated with itself and convinced of an untrammelled potential. The dream of the self-made man and the belief that every man could be a success invaded Canada. It made women uppity and fired young men with heady ambitions. A son could exceed a father, birth did not entirely control destiny, and anyone who truly tried might achieve knighthood and a stone mansion with a *porte cochère.*

A life insurance salesman could become a bank president – George Cox of Peterborough, Ontario, not only became head of the Bank of Commerce but by the end of the decade was president of Canada Life as well.

A country founded on fish, fur and timber was not about to cramp the style of enterprising and sometimes ruthless money men. By the end of the decade six fisheries in British Columbia were bringing in forty-two per cent of the catch, Impe-rial Oil of Sarnia was practically the only supplier of oil in central Canada, and the price of nails could increase suddenly from $1.20 a keg to $2.55 a keg without any explanation required.

On both sides of the border there was talk of one continent, one country, and as a prelude to what some thought would be an inevitable union, American investors were moving into Canada, nudging aside old British money in fast-growth development. In 1899 Charles O. Stillman, scion of a New Jersey oil family, contributed the capital for the Imperial Oil Company to move its refinery from Petrolia, Ontario, the short distance to Sarnia. In return Stillman got a majority of the voting stock.

In Sault Ste. Marie, the townsfolk literally danced around the machinery in the great new pulp mill built by a promoter from Maine, Francis Hector Clergue, who seemed to have more confidence in Canada than Canadians did.

But Canadians were also making canny and sometimes clandestine fortunes. Besides the ever-present bonanzas available in railway building, there were mercantile and milling fortunes to be won. Savings-conscious, cautious wage-earners were creating wealth for banks and insurance companies, and here and there were the high-rollers, men with green thumbs in the money gardens.

Alexander Gibson of New Brunswick, for one,

STRICTLY BUSINESS-LIKE.

Senior Partner *(to head clerk)*—" You'll excuse me for mentioning it, but—er—your face is hardly as tidy as I would like to see it."

Head Clerk—" I'm letting my whiskers grow, sir."

Senior Partner—" So I see; but I can't permit employés to grow their whiskers in business hours. They must do that in their own time ! "

Opposite page: *There are no women among the upstanding clerks at the Laurentide Pulp Mill offices in Grand'Mère, P.Q. Working at high desks under electric lights, clerks earned no more than the men who cut the timber. At this William Van Horne enterprise backed by American and Canadian capital, the language of work was English, not French.*

Victorians concerned with fatigue and loss of vitality sought relief from potions and electric belts and rest cures at sanitariums – a measure of the pace of the '90s rat-race.

was reputedly one of the richest men in the country. He had thousands of employees in an empire which included a railway company, lumber camps, brickyards, canneries and an enormous cotton mill. Henri Mercier, known as the chocolate king of France, bought the entire Anticosti Island for $125,000 and ruled it like a feudal lord. The sixty-two families who happened to be living there at the time of the purchase were forbidden alcohol and guns.

the new tycoons

Robert Simpson and Timothy Eaton, Toronto's rival merchants, did better than two million dollars in business annually. Alexander Ogilvie of Montreal had a grip on flour mills and George Gooderham in Ontario had the world's largest whisky distillery. Montreal's Hugh Graham started a penny newspaper in the 1860s, the *Evening Star*, and by the nineties took in $45,000 a year in profits, a fortune in terms of the day. From his Vancouver shop, C.E. Tisdall sold trout flies to anglers all over the world.

It all rested on a foundation of hard-working men, women and children. Canada's emerging millionaires were paying paltry wages to workers labouring in conditions that killed some of them outright, maimed others, and shortened lives. The labour movement in Canada, still in protracted infancy, was struggling to remedy conditions and incomes but was having its head bloodied for its pains. Wealthy Canadians, following the model of Andrew Carnegie and John D. Rockefeller, found it cheaper to bestow good works than good wages. Universities, concert halls, hospitals and libraries, usually bearing the name of the philanthropist, were rising in Canada's major cities.

William Macdonald, the wealthy and eccentric Montreal tobacco magnate, gave $15 million to McGill University in his lifetime. His instructions

for the engineering building were, "Make everything the very best and send me the bill." He also founded and endowed Macdonald Agricultural College.

Donald Smith and George Stephen (already dubbed Lord Strathcona and Lord Mount Stephen) of CPR fame made Montreal the gift of Victoria Hospital. Each man put in half a million dollars for the building and another million for operating costs. In Toronto, Hart Massey, celebrating the merger of his farm machinery company with that of Alanson Harris, donated a concert hall to the city.

There were earthly rewards for such good-heartedness. Ogilvie, Gooderham, George Drummond, and William Sanford of Hamilton received appointments to the Senate. Others who made conspicuous public bequests were almost assured of a title. The Queen's birthday honour list made Sirs (and Ladies) of politicians, financiers and shop-keepers who, in the eyes of the influential, earned a place in the "new aristocracy."

jewel cases on wheels

High society and the newly rich were unabashedly ostentatious. Railway presidents and others of wealth had private railway cars that were jewel cases on wheels, with crystal chandeliers, velvet upholstered furniture and fresh flowers in crystal vases. The decor provided some solace for the discomfort of train travel over the uneven rail beds. On some stretches of track it was impossible to bathe, the water would not stay in the tub. Passengers would lie in their berths holding tight to the sides as the car pitched from side to side. Those susceptible to motion sickness were in misery, cold cloths on their foreheads, medicinal champagne at hand.

Services and goods were so cheap that even modest incomes were sufficient to purchase the trappings of middle-class substance. A mahogany table at Timothy Eaton's store cost $3.95, a solid oak combination desk and bookcase with a drop lid, brass railing, raised carving and a velvet curtain was $4.85. A man could have a custom-tailored wool suit sewn with silk thread for $11. Hand-stitched, high-button leather shoes for women cost $2. A maid in uniform could be had for an annual wage of $360, keep included.

fringes on everything

It was a period in which clutter was adored. Whatever was sparse, lean and simple and without ornament, seemed in the nineties to indicate a state of pauperism. The drawing room of Sir Casimir Gzowski's Toronto home was a reeling congestion of stuffed owls, photographs in ornate frames, glass paperweights, ostrich eggs, statues, enamelled clocks, peacock plumes, *cloisonné* vases, japanned trays, carved boxes, wax flowers, swagged pillows, and fringes on everything else.

The overall effect was pompous, but not without a certain innocent, unselfconscious charm. The nineties could permit itself an excess of whimsical decor, since everything else was secure. The sensuality of chubby cupids and the prevalence of heliotrope watered silk was above reproach, but behaviour was controlled, sex unmentionable, the family a triumph of virtue and order, and God's purpose understood. The man who built a home ponderous enough to withstand a seige could indulge in a cornice of grinning gargoyles without fear of being called frivolous.

The basic architectural styles of the day were full of mixed messages. Public buildings followed either the Romanesque style or, in some cases, the hot Chicago builders who were constructing skyscrapers ten storeys high, gaining for the Windy City the name of "the cradle of architecture for the continent." Either way, it was apt to result in

Scarcely an inch is unadorned in Mrs. Vaughan's Montreal drawing room. The parlour upright is the focus of these ladies' attention amid the cacophony of silks, figurines and bric-a-brac.

**Gerhard Heintzman
The Piano-maker**

In the 1890s, when competition in the piano, organ and gramophone business was at its peak, the pride of many a Canadian concert hall or parlour was the Heintzman. In 1860 Theodor Heintzman, a cabinet-maker from Germany, arrived in Canada, and a few years later in Toronto opened a piano manufactory. There were several other piano-makers in the area, but business was good. When Gerhard took over the firm, the piano was a standard fixture in most homes: pump organs were a thing of the past, and the player piano was becoming faddish. So too was a gadget called the gramophone, and Heintzman, like others, tried his hand at those as well. But in the end, Heintzman's success was in following his father's line of work, and for decades the classic Canadian piano was the Heintzman.

something that resembled a stone pastry. Doors were massive and rippling with carved leaves, lobbies had marble floors and walls, wide stairways cascaded from tall ceilings. The style of hotel building was of medieval castles. Everything was huge: city halls, department stores, legislative buildings and churches rose like cliffs on streets only recently paved.

People who could afford it consumed enormous meals. Extra weight was regarded fondly as a sign of health and affluence. The bustle was still in vogue at the beginning of the decade but made only a brief come-back before it gave way to the tight-laced styles of the end of the era.

shifting the curves

The demise of the bustle was succeeded by a shift of the enhancing bulk from the lower rear to the bosom and sleeves. Bodices were puffed out over cummerbund cinches and sleeves were bunched in a style known as "leg-of-mutton." One fashion writer observed trillingly, "They are so becoming that it is difficult to imagine ever being able to tolerate small ones again."

Only a few homes could boast of the new steam radiators. In most, the kitchen stove and a fireplace provided the only heat and people awakened in the mornings in frigid bedrooms. Both men and women wore long knit woolen underwear, making a thriving business for textile mills such as Stanfield's in Truro, Nova Scotia.

Hair was piled high over false pieces, a mode immortalized by Charles Dana Gibson's illustrations. Chapeaus as big as tea trays were secured by ten-inch hat pins. The Toronto *Mail's* witty "Kit" described the hat of one woman at the 1895 Queen's Plate as "a majestic creation of roses, vegetables, jet flies and horns."

The purpose of the entire ensemble was to set off waistlines which, despite the fondness for plumpness, were required to measure eighteen inches—or at least appear to. Under the dresses, high-necked in daytime and five yards around the hem, under the haircloth lining which extended to the knees in order to ensure that movement would not reveal the shape of thighs, and under the petticoats, was a waist-pinching corset so restricting that women sometimes fainted, or "swooned," from inability to breathe.

In the evening young women defied their shocked elders and displayed bare arms and a thoroughly immodest neckline. There was a fad for capes of sable with matching hats trimmed with the head and paws of the animal.

Men's clothing, on the other hand, was neatly conservative. The long, graceful frock coats worn by the stylish since Confederation were giving way to short, terse jackets worn with lean pressed trousers. Men still wore tailcoats on formal occasions but a new tail-less jacket, the tuxedo imported by members of New York's swank Tuxedo Country Club, was catching on. Beards and bushy sideburns and even the moustache had a dated look: fashionable men were clean-shaven and their hair was cropped short.

foreign styles on top

High society was middle-class, left to merchants and their wives who were, in the main, untravelled and unsure. The vogue was taken from London for men, from Paris for the ladies. The women spent their afternoons in carriages. In Vancouver, they promenaded through Stanley Park, in Halifax they took the air at the Public Gardens, near Quebec they went to look at Montmorency Falls, in Montreal they wrapped themselves in sable robes in winter, in Toronto they nodded politely as they passed on Jarvis Street. They could judge the cost of a new carriage or the worth of a pair of chestnuts as accurately as an auctioneer.

Stereoscopes

On wintry evenings, couples could curl up before the fire and imagine "going with the stream."

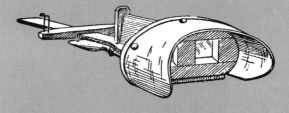

Stereoscopic photography was a wonder in its day, and no late-nineteenth century parlour was complete without a stereoscope. The technique was simple but the effect was grand. Two photos were taken of the same scene at slightly different angles. Mounted side by side and viewed through the stereoscope, they produced a three dimensional image that brought Niagara Falls tumbling into the viewer's lap and sent the Rockies towering away into the distance. Stereoscopes came in a wide variety of subjects: wonders of the world, comic studio scenes, distant battles, history-making events. Before motion pictures destroyed the market, one English supplier boasted over one million selections. What better excuse could one find to linger on the porch or snuggle in the hammock with one's beau or belle?

Sabre-tooth tigers, wolves, foxes and martens leapt out of this scene at Laliberté's Fur Parlor, Quebec.

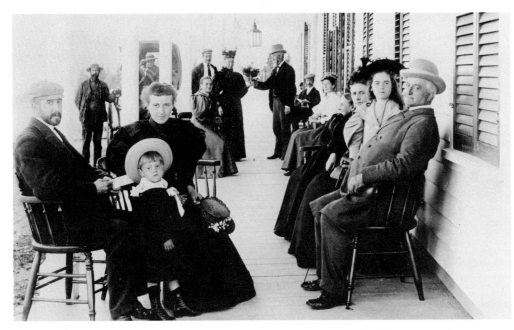

Posed and attired in their Sunday best, a Quebec family – from grandchildren to grandparents – gathers on the hotel verandah at Tadoussac near Quebec. Even the carriage driver has managed to get into the picture (above). Across the river at Cacouna (below), the family is in mourning, but it looks like uncle is going boating anyway. Even at resorts people dressed from head to toe.

Horse-talk dominated many social gatherings. People rode to the hounds at the London Hunt Club in imitation of Devon squires; women were obliged to ride side-saddle. Outstanding social events of the season included horse races, the Queen's Plate at Toronto's Woodbine track being the pinnacle.

The arrival of the gentry at one Queen's Plate was described in the *Mail and Empire*: "Ragged little girls stood on the sidewalk and watched with wondering eyes the beautifully dressed women ride by in their carriages; vulgar little boys took vast amusement from the commoners who clung to the street cars almost by their teeth . . . ."

cottage country

The country's prosperous could afford two homes, one near a lake to escape the sultry summers in the cities. Toronto society chose property in the Lake Simcoe and Muskoka Lakes regions. Those who couldn't afford a summer villa lived in tents or lightly constructed frame shelters and sang around campfires at night. Montreal society adjourned to Murray Bay and Cacouna; a few mixed with Americans who were making their summer homes in the Thousand Islands.

The craze for summer residences rapidly drove up prices. Islands in Muskoka which had once gone for fifty cents an acre could command over $11 an acre in 1897. New Brunswick's salmon streams were being sold to Americans, Englishmen and a few Canadians for sums as great as $6,000! Cottage life soon became less rustic. Glorious gingerbread palaces were built, some with room for fifty guests. Gardeners tended shrubbery and uniformed maids served tea in latticed pagodas on manicured lawns. At Baie des Châleurs the vogue was chalets of pine logs, with adjoining servants' quarters, stable and laundry.

The ultimate social insult was to be called

"provincial" – one unacquainted with the dictates of manners and etiquette; a boor who laughed loudly, used slang, had casual attitudes and didn't know the rules. Books on etiquette were best-sellers, particularly Emily Holt's definitive *Encyclopaedia of Etiquette: What to Write, What to Wear, What to Do, What to Say, A Book of Manners for Everyday Use.* Dorothy Dix and Beatrice Fairfax had advice columns in the daily newspapers dealing with such worrisome problems as the proper boarding of carriages and length of gloves to be worn to afternoon tea.

Lady Kirkpatrick, wife of Ontario's lieutenant governor, ruled Toronto's society by being haughtier than anyone else in town. Society was absorbed in a pastime as complicated and challenging as chess, the formal call. "Ladies" suffered considerable anxiety selecting their "days" and times for an "at home". Lady Kirkpatrick of Toronto claimed Wednesday. Guests, announced by a butler, were received in the ballroom where they shook hands with the hostess, accepted one cup of tea, (two at the most!) and departed within a half hour. Only the hostess shook hands: all other women greeted each other with "a studied inclination of the head, a very fleeting smile, and a murmur of the name."

visiting under wraps

Women did not remove their veils, gloves or wraps when calling. Refreshments which might cause "unpleasant consequences to the gloves" were avoided. When a woman rose to leave, every man in the room rose to his feet. Men of breeding never stood in front of their chairs but slighly to one side or directly behind. It *mattered.*

Callers were not necessarily restricted to the designated days. Younger men and women, women married to men on the way up, or women married to men slipping out of favour, visited their betters freely, knowing full well they would not lay

eyes on the chatelaine. The point of the exercise was to leave a calling card, a testament of being someone of almost-equal status. The *crème de la crème* only called when circumstances of consequence demanded.

Although a gentleman's card could bear his military rank or any title, no other embellishment was proper. A lady's never bore her address. The cards introduced an unspoken code that involved turning down the appropriate corner. A left-hand upper corner meant felicitations, left-hand lower corner, condolences; the right-hand lower corner, "to take leave," and the right-hand upper corner turned down meant "delivered in person."

card-carrying in style

The cards were medium weight bristol board, with only a slight sheen, and the name was engraved in black ink. Clerks and seamstresses could afford them and did, carrying them in ornamented cases and proferring them with a delicious sense of importance.

In such an age of rigidity, romantic novels provided outlets for cribbed imaginations. A rage in Canada in 1897 was *The Turkish Messiah* by Israel Zangwill. A typical passage read:

Her white teeth flashed twixt laughing lips. His voice was hoarse, faltering. This new sense of romance that, like a callow-bird, had been stirring in his breast ever since he had heard of her quest for him, spread its wings and soared heavenwards . . . She came nearer and her eyes wrapped him in flame. "My Prince!" she cried.

To be sure, a proper marriage followed speedily.

That was the stuff: burning but chaste love, love conquering some insurmountable obstacle, often a difference in social class. There was a rags to riches triumph and a payoff for purity in every ending.

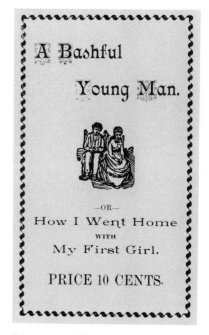

There's no telling the misfortunes that might befall a bashful young man if on the night he first meets Annie, the girl of his dreams, foul weather prevents their parting. Not enough to face her gruff father in the morning! but to sit on one's beaver hat and cough in one's coffee and overturn the table and be chased by a bull . . . the mortifications and more . . . all for the price of 10¢.

Tekahionwake
Princess of Flint and Feather

She was the greatest show business one-night stand in the country, but she died almost broke. Every high school pupil has read at least one of her poems, but the real Pauline Johnson was quite different from the myth. She was born in 1862 on Ontario's Six Nations reserve and given the name Tekahionwake, "the smokey haze of late summer." At an early age she took an interest in poetry, but her stage debut did not come until she was 30. She toured the country from Port aux Basques to Victoria, packing opera houses, drawing rooms and town saloons. A beautiful, quick-witted woman, she was proud of her heritage and wore her Mohawk costume at her recitals. When an old dowager once asked if her father was really an Indian, she quipped, "Was your father really a white man?" *Flint and Feather* (1912) appeared a year before her death.

In the nineties Canadians went to see plays with such titles as *Two Orphans, Lost in London*, and *Drink*, the latter described by critics as the finest melodrama written in twenty-five years. Mrs. John Drew was adored, a smash hit in *The Road to Ruin* though she was in her seventies. James O'Neill, father of American dramatist Eugene O'Neill, was locked in his fate as the Count of Monte Cristo. Sir Henry Irving came to Toronto in *Beckett*, creating such excitement that scalpers got thirteen dollars a ticket, an amout equal to a maid's wages for a month. Thomas W. Keane toured as Shylock and shook the stage with his pole-axed fall in the trial scene, and Maurice Barrymore played Hamlet with liquid eyes and his hand on his heart.

Audiences doted on performing authors. Indian poet Pauline Johnson was the darling of the country, wearing full tribal deerskins and a doomed expression as she recited her poetry. James Whitcomb Riley, the richest author on the continent, was a hit with his readings from *The Old Swimmin' Hole* and *'leven More Poems*. Mark Twain was still active touring occasionally, making laconic asides as he delivered paragraphs from *Huckleberry Finn*.

outdoor, pocket circuses

Canadians also delighted in medicine shows, actually pocket circuses staged on outdoor stages dramatically lit by gasoline torches, or P.T. Barnum's freaks and sleepy man-eating tigers, or aging Buffalo Bill Cody's sideshows. Tumblers, magicians and a fireworks display titled "The Storming of the Bastille" drew thousands at fall fairs that marked the end of the harvest.

In winter toboggan chutes coated in ice were built wherever river banks were steep enough, offering a heart-stopping ride for the daring. At night the revelers were an enchanting spectacle, illuminated by bonfires and Chinese lanterns. The most famous winter carnival in the country was held at Quebec City every February. The highlight was the midnight storming of an ice fort by hundreds of people on snowshoes, each holding a torch or roman candle.

Most families made their own entertainment, particularly in winter in isolated farm homes. Some played fiddles, some told stories, and most everyone could sing, or tried. An early grounding in parlour recitations and Sunday School pageants resulted in a generation of adults and children who could perform unselfconsciously. Adults tended to turn most public and social occasions into fancy-dress affairs.

the great dress ball

One of the most successful gatherings of the era was the Historical Dress Ball the governor general and his wife, Lord and Lady Aberdeen, gave in 1896 in Ottawa. They used the Senate Chamber for the occasion and assigned roles to each guest. Ottawa society was in a dither and rehearsed for weeks in advance, driving Montreal dressmakers to distraction with their demands. Members of parliament, cabinet ministers, judges, ambassadors and senators, together with wives and children flung themselves with abandon into the enterprise. The event began with Viking songs and dances, followed by the landing of Cabot (wearing the costume of a Venetian fop), the departure of Jacques Cartier from the court of Francis I, after which Acadiens danced a merry quadrille and so on. (The governor general and his wife knew their Canadian history, more or less).

The same infatuation for costume was evidenced in the regalia worn by organizations, social, religious or recreational. The more somber ones worn by the Salvation Army or the Boys' Brigade (an early attempt to combat juvenile delinquency) were modelled on the military. Some fraternal organizations like the Shriners preferred a Persian harem motif, with satin pantaloons and tasselled fez. Men of military rank turned out in dress uniform; their ladies donned white gowns with a diagonal ribbon from shoulder to hip.

Diamond Jubilee year

In 1897, Queen Victoria's Diamond Jubilee year, communities built preposterous archways along their main streets and staged the best parade of their lives. There were patriotic speeches by day, bonfires and fireworks and military bands by night. In Montreal the Windsor Hotel celebrated by installing thousands of lights over its facade. People so packed the street to stare at the awesome sight that traffic could not move.

The Diamond Jubilee parade in London, Ontario, was typical of that summer. Led by one hundred men on decorated bicycles, the assemblage was heralded by the 7th Battalion Band, 50 members of the Ancient Order of United Workmen, 100 from the Independent Order of Foresters, 128 marchers from the Canadian Order of Chosen Friends, followed by the 27th Battalion Band, then 20 Grand United Order Oddfellows, 60 Canadian Order Oddfellows, the 32nd Battalion Band, the Musical Society Band, 300 Ancient Order Foresters, after which came 160 Juvenile Foresters, a fife and drum band, 200 Orangemen, the 26th Battalion Band, some members of the Irish Benevolent Society, and bringing up the glorious rear, the mayor, aldermen, school trustees and firemen.

As a warm darkness fell on the exhausted town that evening, fireworks spelling VICTORIA hung for a long, poignant moment in the black sky. People watched it sputter out and were transfixed. It seemed something important had happened to them, to the whole country. It felt like a flowering, a future greatness just opening to enfold them all.

He was billed EDWARD BEAUPRÉ, GÉANT, *and at the sideshow he was the biggest attraction around. Born in Willow Bunch, Sask., at the height of his career he was 8'2" tall and wore a size 24 shoe.*

Giving An At-Home

A cartoonist takes a satirical swipe at the high-society highlight of the social season – giving an "at-home." "The courageous hostess endeavouring to give an 'at-home' must be well acquainted with the rules of etiquette and employ servants equally attuned. The slightest slight, the most innocent ignorance will send ripples that will surely return. At the first sound of the bell, a servant should attend the door. When announcing guests, pronounce the names distinctly, adding an agreeable embellishment, such as "an old and valued friend." The latest arrival takes the seat left vacant near the hostess. Light cakes and tea are expected, and a suitable entertainment should be provided, piano music or a recitation, perhaps. When visitors retire, accompany them as far to the door as the circumstances of your friendship demand. You may expect personal calls of appreciation within a month's time.

HOW TO SQUARE YOUR SOCIAL ACCOUNT: A FEW HINTS FOR THE INEXPERIENCED.

Ask all you can. They will nearly all come.

Let your servants make what they can out of it. It reconciles them to lowish wages.

A few judicious introductions are advisable.

Have songs in the inner drawing-room, and endeavour to prevent talking during their continuance.

Some arrangement for the men's hats and coats is necessary.

Provide light refreshments. (This is absolutely essential, and your friends will gladly get them as best they can.)

Ales, wines and liquors flowed freely in the nineties despite temperance and prohibition crusades. Tossed into the street outside the tavern, a fallen-down drunk is helped by a wealthy samaritan. Social reformers, mostly from the well-to-do, gradually began to show some concern for the poor and the derelict.

CHAPTER TWO

Living Recklessly

I am a temperance woman. No one can realize more than I the devastation and ruin alcohol in its many tempting forms has brought. . . .

Light on Dark Corners, 1894

Hard drink was the legacy of the frontier, of cod-fishing fleets making summer stopovers in the coves, of voyageurs fueling themselves with brandy for cruel portages, and the edge-of-nowhere panic of refugees from Highland crofts and Dublin slums. It was still a nervous and new country, and booze offered release from toil and terror. There was booze in patent medicine for women's complaints, booze in milk to quiet the baby, booze wherever men congregated. The poor were drowning in it. Montreal reformer Herbert Brown Ames studied poverty in a working class district of Montreal where a quarter of the families lived on less than five dollars a week. He counted 105 saloons and 78 grocery shops that sold liquor, which he judged to represent one liquor outlet for every thirty-three families.

Hard drinking and colourful, rugged parlance carried over to political meetings which were virtually stag parties since women could not vote. Halls were packed with unbathed men, the air thick with smoke, spittoons scattered everywhere, admonitions to use them growing dingy on the walls. Whiskey jugs were passed from hand to hand, each man giving it a sharp shake to distribute the sediment evenly before taking a fiery swallow.

A Conservative cabinet minister, George Foster, was called a "slimy eel of hell" by a Liberal. The *Labor Advocate* once warned voters against an aspiring school trustee by declaring him "an enemy of mankind as well as a notorious scab baker."

Men travelled for miles to hear political speeches, a rousing and welcome diversion in a country where most of the population farmed. The hustings abounded with politicians who could rise to the occasion and talk for hours without referring to a note or repeating an insult, every sentence richly ornamented with curls of adjectives and garlands of adverbs.

Some were also witty, and none more so than John A. Macdonald. He was sitting on a platform one evening while an opponent discussed at great length the prime minister's moral and administrative infirmities. When it came his turn to speak, John A. stood a moment in reflective silence. With the hall hushed in expectancy, he sighed and observed with comfortable satisfaction, "What an old devil I am!"

Charles Tupper, recalled from London and his post of Canadian High Commissioner to lead the Conservative government in its ill-fated campaign of 1896, had a reputation for making excessive use of the first person singular in his speeches. At one raucous occasion in Massey Hall in Toronto, Lib-

" What ll you drink, McDougall ? "
" I don't know, what'll *you* drink ? "
" I think I'll have a pale ale."
" Well, I'll have a pail of ale, too."

And did you hear the one about the minister finishing his sermon: "Oh, my brethren, hell is a terrible place! It is the abode of fiery spirits and . . ." Old Soak (interrupting): "Hold on! You're describing heaven."

Grip

**Joseph Israel Tarte
"Judas Iscariot"**

In 1891 he marched into the House of Commons, a black bag under his arm; when its contents was made public, Hector Langevin, minister of public works, and MP Thomas McGreevy were ousted from office. The exposé earned Tarte the title "Judas Iscariot": both the men he accused and he were Conservatives. Whatever his motives, the Tories never forgave him. Joseph Israel Tarte was the son of a Quebec farmer, born in 1848 in Lanoraie. He worked as a notary before he turned to journalism and politics. After his defection he sat with the Liberals, and in the election of 1896 was instrumental in the party victory. Ironically perhaps, Laurier appointed him minister of public works. In 1902, however, he was dismissed for opposing the party's policies and returned to manage and edit his newspaper, *La Patrie,* in support of the Tories.

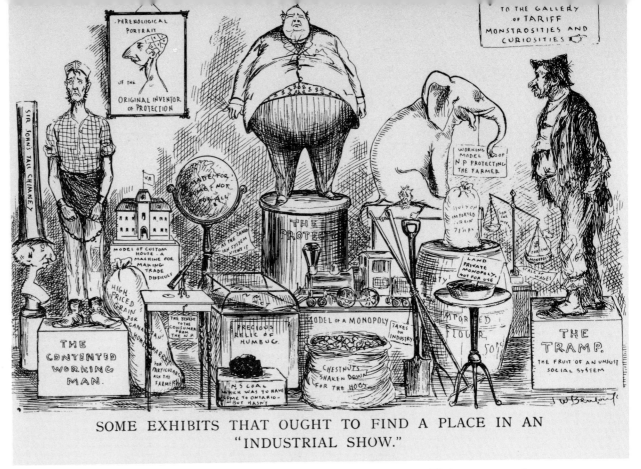

SOME EXHIBITS THAT OUGHT TO FIND A PLACE IN AN "INDUSTRIAL SHOW."

Cartoonist J. W. Bengough, a free-trader, blamed John A.'s policy of protective tariffs for poverty and tramps.

erals in the audience sent up such a thunderously derisive chant of "I,I,I,I" that a reporter ten feet away could not hear a word Tupper was shouting.

Elections were as larcenous as they were exuberant, as riotous as the politicians were eloquent, despite sporadic reform movements. In nearby London, Ontario, town drunks and indigents formed a raffish parade to the door of Nellie Edwards' grandfather's home. Every man received two dollars from grandfather Edwards to vote for the Grits. His wife's comment on the transactions was to sweep the doorstep fiercely after each departure. Important men came by dark of night, muffled, to confer secretly in the parlour. The children were warned to tell no one about their visits, and especially not their uncle John, a Tory, who

lived next door. It did not present a serious problem in discretion, since the families stopped speaking during elections anyway.

Election strategies included ballot burning, ballot switching, ballot stuffing, voter impersonation, voter intimidation, and forms of bribery ranging from straight to bent. Winners and losers were occupied equally after the election with unseatment petitions, recounts, mysterious appearances of lost ballot boxes, mysterious disappearances of crucial ballot boxes, and accusations of treachery and malfeasance, usually well-founded. Disputes dragged on for weeks, stalling governments in thickets of uncertainty.

It seemed to many Canadians that such disorder, uproar and villainy was natural to the political

26

JIM EDGAR'S PROTEST

EDGAR—"I said I could lick you, Dudey Caron, an' so I kin, just as easy as rollin' off a log. But I never said I could do it with one hand, an' I ain't agoin' to try, not if your gang yells 'Coward' till they bust."

Political scandals and charges of "boodling" rocked politics as "honourable members" openly called each other crooks.

Thomas McGreevy "Uncle"

When Thomas McGreevy was ousted from the House in 1892, *Grip*'s "Gallery of Notables" printed the following political obituary: "Mr. McGreevy has never done anything for the country (so far as we know). He sat in Parliament to represent his own pocket . . . and no man ever performed that mission with greater ability." The slang term for it was "uncle-ing," and "Uncle" McGreevy was caught in the act. Some years before he had loaned his friend, Hector Langevin, $35,000. When the latter became Tory minister of public works, McGreevy was on the Quebec Harbour Commission, and together they arranged for a $3.1 million contract with a firm employing McGreevy's brother. The take for Thomas was supposed to be $172,000, but MP Israel Tarte (left) exposed the fraud. Criminal charges ruined him, and he died penniless.

process, since none had ever known an election that was otherwise. But there was a growing intolerance of some of the more flagrant abuses. The Toronto *Globe*, for instance, reported that candidates in the 1896 federal election had announced as part of their campaign speeches the amount of money they were offering for a vote. Toronto's *Saturday Night*, which often took unusual editorial positions, urged its readers to register their disapproval of political chicanery by stating on their ballots that they supported neither candidate.

It was relatively uncommon for protest to succeed. Joseph Israel Tarte, a life-long Conservative who saw no contradiction in serving Liberal leader Wilfrid Laurier as well, launched in the early 1890s a purge of prominent Tories. Hector Lan-

gevin, minister of public works for twenty years, was obliged to resign in 1891, and Thomas McGreevy, MP for Quebec West, was later sent to jail. Tarte's informant, a New Yorker named Owen E. Murphy, told the *New York Times:* "The Langevin crowd is worse than the Tweed gang ever was." (William Marcy "Boss" Tweed and his Tammany Hall cronies defrauded New York City of well over $100 million from 1862 to 1871.) Tarte was dubbed "Judas Iscariot" by less than grateful Tories.

After the election of 1896 put the Liberals in power, the *Milton Reformer* announced that the town certainly would not get a new post office: Milton had elected a Tory.

Certainly the prevalence of "boodling," as

The modern game of tennis was but twenty years old when these fashionable club members (above) in sports clothes, ties, caps and leather shoes took to the court in Calgary for a doubles match. Hockey had no need of private clubs or fees. All that was needed was a curved stick – a willow branch would do – and a frozen Saskatchewan slough (below), and even the girls could join in.

kickbacks were called, owed something to the heady competition that was thriving in business, politics and sport in the nineties. Spectators turned out by the hundreds to cheer hockey, lacrosse and rugby football.

The newly formed Amateur Hockey Association had just begun organizing the game. Two sons of Lord Stanley, the governor general until 1893, played for the Rideau Hall Rebels and many believe it was their influence that prompted Lord Stanley to donate a $50 sterling silver bowl as the premier prize among amateur hockey teams across the country. The Montreal Amateur Athletic Association defeated Ottawa 3–1 on March 22, 1894 to win the first Stanley Cup. There were no nets in the goals to stop the puck, the players didn't wear gloves and the referee wore ordinary clothes and a bowler hat. Women enjoyed playing the game and took part in vigorous matches from the rinks of Montreal to the frozen sloughs of Saskatchewan.

Boxing matches provided another source of vicarious and participatory stimulation. Bareknuckle fights were rarely seen any more, replaced by "glove fights" but the weight of the gloves varied from lightly padded to lethal skin-tight ones.

the first black champion

John L. Sullivan was the heavyweight champion and the controversial Marquess of Queensbury rules had been widely adopted. Purists disgustedly claimed the rules had despoiled the virility of the contests but the record of George "Little Chocolate" Dixon from Halifax belies the assessment.

The first black man to win a world boxing championship (in fact he held two), Dixon knocked out Nunc Wallace in 1890 to win the world bantamweight title and $2,000. He won the featherweight title a year later. His first major fight was with Cal McCarthy in Boston. The two men battled, wearing two ounce gloves, for an inhuman seventy rounds. Following four and a half hours, they agreed to a draw. In one year Dixon fought three twenty-five round fights, three at twenty, one at ten and three at six.

blood in the press

Newspapers, sometimes even the sports pages, reeked with blood and gore. William Randolph Hearst and Joseph Pulitzer had launched yellow journalism in the United States with such impressive results on circulation that many Canadian papers took it up. *Massey's Magazine* complained in 1896 about this creeping Americanism, noting with regret that "most of the newspapers of the country prefer to emulate their depraved contemporaries on the other side of the line to adopting the staid tone of the press of Great Britain."

Much of the lustiness of the age was the product of saturation drinking which prevailed. Since mid-century, middle class Protestant men and women had promoted temperance, concerned that the country was drinking itself to death. Now they were organized prohibitionists and were starting to dry up the countryside with legislation.

Lady Aberdeen, wife of the governor general of Canada from 1893 to 1898, was astounded by the quantity of alcohol consumed by Ottawa's leading citizens at a New Year's Day levee. She noted that the ladies were no more restrained than the men. She was particularly dismayed at the sight of the country's elite vaulting over a table that obstructed their path to the cloakroom.

When the House of Commons sat for five continuous days and nights to debate the Remedial Bill of 1896 that would dispose of the Manitoba school question, the bar never closed. The member for Assiniboia entertained in the smoking room by performing a ceremonial dance of the Blackfoot tribe, which he followed with a jig down the length of the refreshment table.

The heaviest drinking occurred in the tent towns that moved with the railway builders or mushroomed around silver or gold strikes. Sandon, settled in British Columbia in 1892 near a silver vein that soon vanished, had twenty-four hotels and twenty-three saloons while the boom lasted. The hotels had steam heat and electric lights, bells to summon bellhops, hot and cold running water in every room, and solid oak furniture. Miners seeking a change of scene would board the train to Spokane on Saturday nights, drinking and playing poker all the way, and return late on Sunday in a stupored silence.

Another British Columbia town, Atlin, close to the Klondike, swelled to a population of ten thousand almost overnight in 1898. There were so many people that the main street was impassable, night and day. The bars never closed because, as the *Atlin Claim* explained, the northern latitude resulted in clocks and watches being "a little uncertain."

kidnapped the premier

Mineral strikes in British Columbia and the Yukon attracted the ambitious and the adventuresome, but also the cracked and crooked. In such company most eccentrics passed unnoticed but the exploits of "Pot-Hole" Kellie were singular even in the flamboyant town of Lardeau City. Pot-Hole once kidnapped the premier of the province, bundled him into a closed carriage and planted him in the middle of a hall where ferocious miners were discussing how much they detested the premier's new mining legislation. When the meeting was over the premier was released. He tottered home and soon after introduced a new mining bill.

Vancouver's founding fathers were the most beseiged men in the West. Drifters, fugitives and

As far back as the 1890s, breweries were already establishing the strong association between beer and sports. The Dominion Brewery supplied curlers with these handy scorecards, with a subtle reminder that after the last rock nothing hit the spot like a bottle of White Label.

ACADEMY OF MUSIC, - HALIFAX, N. S.

THREE NIGHTS, Commencing

Thursday, — AUG. 18

" TO REFUSE THAT MAN A DRINK OF LIQUOR IS A CRIME."

THE MOST TALKED ABOUT PLAY OF THE AGE

THE VOLUNTEER ORGANIST

A TEMPERANCE LESSON IN DRAMATIC FORM.

Halifax teetotallers and temperance advocates packed the Academy of Music for this uplifting lesson in 1898. Around the corner and down the street, grog shops did brisk competitive business.

other dispossessed turned the city into a non-stop poker party. In 1886, when the community was a year old, the population was about 5,000. Clearly few were family men, since only fifty-eight of that number were children. Gangs of thugs roamed the streets, robbing drunks sleeping in the mud. Corpses with stab wounds in their backs could be found hidden in the weeds. The streets were lined with a jovial mix of brothels, opium dens, saloons and gambling houses, against which Methodist missionaries flailed in vain.

opium smugglers ruined

Opium was legal, and Vancouver was head-quarters for Canada's importers. When the governor general and his wife arrived there for a formal visit, their agenda included an inspection of an opium factory. The Aberdeens were favourably impressed. Lady Aberdeen commented cynically that it was unfortunate that the United States had removed its import tax on opium and thereby ruined a number of Canadian smugglers.

Vancouver was also headquarters for "yellow slaves," as the Victorians called young Chinese women forced into prostitution. A Methodist clergyman in Vancouver was waging a campaign to rescue Chinese girls brought to Canada, "for the wrong purposes."

Gusto, gangsters and all, Vancouver boomed. Its population tripled in six years. Citizens spent $27,000 a year for liquor licences alone, and four breweries worked around the clock to keep up with demand. Mine operators, beset with absenteeism after Sunday drinking sprees, were advocating a seven-day work week.

Patrolling the great expanse between Manitoba and the Rockies, the North-West Mounted Police, a hard drinking lot themselves, were disgusted to find that a major part of their activities was the enforcement of unenforceable liquor laws. The tingling side of the business was watching the flat sky-line for a dust trail that would reveal the presence of a bootlegger from the Dakotas. The Mounties found it distasteful to open suspicious bundles on railway trains and check "topers" in the saloons for their permits. After 1875, permits were required to import liquor into the North-West Territories and even then for "medicinal or sacramental use only."

The Mounties pleaded with Ottawa to abandon the liquor laws. Their authority to search private homes for liquor without a warrant was a particular cause for resentment in the North-West Territories, and exposed them to accusations of hypocrisy—particularly after H Troop got so drunk in Lethbridge after receiving some back pay that the whole town was terrorized.

In 1891 the federal government yielded slightly to the Mounties' complaints and turned over liquor control to the Territories' legislature. Laws promptly became more permissive, which appalled neighbouring Manitoba. The temperance movement, imported from Ontario and the United States in the 1880s, promptly hardened. Manitobans began demanding nothing less than total prohibition in their province.

Manitoba goes dry

The favourite targets of local dries were the small frame hotels that stood next to the CPR station in every town on the line. The hotel's financial backbone was the long mahogany bar, buffed to a glossy sheen, fitted with a brass rail to put a boot on and stocked with a row of handy spittoons. To the dismay of the women folk, the Mounties took their obligation to supervise the licences of such bars very casually. In 1892 Manitoba took action, held a plebiscite and voted itself dry.

Nothing changed. There was no precedent in Canadian history and the issue went all the way to

While prohibitionists in other parts of the city and country railed against the evil of drink, these Montreal passers-by tried to guess how many gulps this giant bottle of cognac would yield.

Grip publisher and cartoonist, J. W. Bengough, toured the nation in the nineties giving "chalk talks" on his favourite topics: women's suffrage, free trade and the evils of alcohol.

the Privy Council in England for a decision as to its constitutionality. When the adjudication came back, no one could understand it. The province hired one of the country's best lawyers, Edward Blake, to divine its meanings. His report, however, was equally incomprehensible and booze continued to flow in Manitoba.

Women had a large stake in prohibition. There were countless cases of men beating their wives following drinking bouts. In Belmont, Manitoba, neighbours once tarred and feathered a conspicuous offender, but much abuse passed unnoticed. Alcohol's effect on the economy was easier to see; farms were falling to pieces, banks were refusing loans to farmers who drank.

In 1898, to fulfil an election promise designed to woo the temperance vote, the Laurier government ordered the country's only nationwide plebiscite on prohibition. Despite the fact that only men could vote, every province outside Quebec voted dry. The vote in British Columbia was closest: 5,731 to 4,756. There was something of a landslide for prohibition in the Maritimes and in Manitoba.

On a head-count only 13,687 more Canadians favoured prohibition than opposed it. By Liberal arithmetic only twenty-three percent of all eligible voters supported prohibition. Thereby, Wilfrid Laurier declared that the plebiscite had failed.

Prohibitionists in Manitoba had to content themselves with making life more difficult for drinkers, something the temperance movement had already accomplished in small towns and stable neighbourhoods all over Canada. Heavy drinking was becoming a conspicuous, unacceptable activity. In 1895 a thirsty visitor to Toronto, Douglas Sladen, wrote "the blight of the Prohibition Act hung over all the festivities which generally consisted of tea and fruit and confectionary and ice cream and introductions." The head of the Canadian National Exhibition civilly offered Sladen a drink of rye, which they consumed together in a broom closet.

A generation of men became skilled at sneaking a drink, putting it down neat in one gulp and replacing the bottle in a bottom drawer before the drink hit their stomachs. But small boys promised their mothers that liquor would never touch their lips, girls vowed never to kiss them if it did. School children put their hands on their hearts and took The Pledge.

The prohibitionists did not even quail in the presence of the governor general himself. When the Aberdeens unloaded their belongings at Cascapedia, Quebec, one summer day, preparing to establish themselves for the season at a nearby lodge, a group of angry women gathered around them. Their wrath was directed at some liquor boxes, which the governor general explained contained only household goods. To prove it he unpacked a few, while his wife held her breath in fear that he would happen upon the wrong ones.

George Green, the proud owner of the Hoffman House in Rossland, B.C., stands at right, below this "pornographic" painting (knee and shoulder exposed!). This bar had all a hard-drinking miner could ask for: brass rail, spittoons for tobacco chewers and Bass Ale on tap. Green even cashed cheques and took in laundry.

The Brewer's Art

The brew-master's art had changed little over the years since Louis Hébert opened the first brewery in Quebec in 1627, but the number of breweries across the country had increased by leaps and bounds. Every town of any size had at least one, and a burgeoning city like Vancouver could boast 29 breweries for its 25,000 population. By decade's end, Canadians were quaffing almost four gallons per person per year – a gallon more than in the previous decade. Brewing was big business, stiff competition was the name of the game, and established firms, some almost a century old, adopted colour advertising and printed colour labels to sell their best ales and lagers. In a tavern or hotel, grandpa would have seen ads like these.

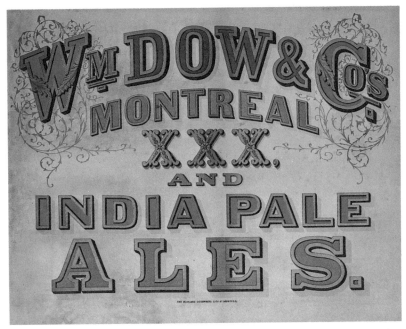

William Dow started in the brewing business back in 1818 in Montreal and opened his first brewery in 1830 – Molson's fiercest competitor in the city.

There are no ladies present in the drawing room as these gents compare the merits of Labatt's Extra Stock, India Pale (two gold medals!) and Stout.

In typical period advertising style, the Toronto Brewing and Malting Company's trade sign would have been proudly displayed over the bar of any number of Toronto taverns and hotels. All bars were "stand-up" then – polished mahogany or walnut – and bar-tenders, starched and spiffy, ready to serve your pleasure.

The husband makes his mark and the homestead is mortgaged, the gravity of the moment etched in the faces of three generations in this George Reid painting. Hard times in the nineties forced many foreclosures, and pioneers who had optimistically settled in the West in the previous decade moved to the U.S.

Hard Times

They run what are known as sweating shops . . . making quite a pile of money and have a few slaves under them in the shape of women. . . .

Witness, Royal Commission on Labour, 1890

Part of the problem was the weather. In the nineties summer came early with a parching, pitiless heat. On the prairies American homesteaders who had moved to the last cheap arable land in the West, moved back again to the U.S. North-West Mounted Police commissioner Lawrence W. Herchmer reported to Ottawa in 1895: "Some districts which were once well settled are now deserted, and in others there are only two or three settlers left."

As the dust gathered on the Prairies, financial panics and sudden contractions of credit, usually sparked by the New York market, caused Canadian businesses to fold like houses of cards. Factories closed and boarded up their windows, sad and eyeless as gravestones. Men tramped the countryside desperate for work.

Tariffs jealously guarded each side of the 49th parallel – farm products were effectively cut off from American markets. Canadians were forced to buy more expensive "Made in Canada" manufactured goods. High shipping costs on the Atlantic made it difficult to sell wheat abroad. Maritimers and Westerners railed against a perennial sore point – high freight rates.

The early nineties demanded a high price for being a Canadian and a great number chose not to pay. By water and rail, Maritimers travelled the routes to Boston and New York. French-Canadians could land jobs for the whole family in Massachusetts textile mills; there were already whole communities of Franco-Americans in Buffalo and Detroit. There were jobs just a stroll away with better wages, better working conditions, more excitement and better prospects.

Canadians joked "What are the only two books in the Old Testament that describe Canada? Answer: Lamentations and Exodus."

The loss to the country was staggering. In 1891 the country could count less than five million citizens. One *million* had gone to the United States in the preceding decade, and another half million left during the economic dip in the nineties. To lose one in every ten Canadians in the exodus was grievous enough but, more significantly, those who uprooted themselves tended to be the ones with the most independent, impatient natures. Those who remained had tenacious ties to farms they had cursed and loved for too long to leave, or believed in continuity, or had pride in a British home, or were too consumed by the difficulties of mere survival to care.

Perhaps some of the advantages of the American connection could be won without leaving home. Some Canadians envisioned a commercial union with the United States, a type of common

In John A.'s last election campaign in 1891, the biggest election issue was the National Policy of tariffs. Propaganda cartoons like this one, circulated by the Industrial League, a front for Canadian manufacturers, painted a picture of shared profits inside the policy's protective wall.

The Ward in Toronto's University and College area was the city's worst slum. Many tumbledown houses like this had no plumbing, and kids played between the outhouse and back fence.

market, while preserving separate governments. The idea of an economic union with the United States so appealed to the Liberal Party that it adopted a version of it in its "unrestricted reciprocity" platform for the 1891 election. Some Canadians and some Americans wanted to go further and faster, hoping for outright annexation. Goldwin Smith saw this as the only solution in *Canada and the Canadian Question*, published just after the 1891 election:

The idea of a United Continent of North America, securing free trade and intercourse over a vast area, with external safety and internal peace, is no less practical than it is grand.

But the election had shown that it wasn't practical politics. Declaring the Liberal platform to be a form of "veiled treason," old John A. had wrapped himself in the Union Jack and from every platform declared, "A British subject I was born, a British subject I will die." "Ottawa, Not Washington Our Capital" the Tory posters read. "The Old Man, the Old Flag, the Old Policy." In vain, the Liberals protested their loyalty and accused the Tories of making Canada such a poor country that the U.S. was annexing Canadians who voted with their feet.

Loyalty to the Canadian dream won in 1891 but did not alter the harsh reality. Hard times continued for another five years.

perpetual debt

The urban poor had a grim time. Much employment was seasonal, shovelling snow in winter and working on the docks in the summer. In between, families missed mortgage payments and ran up food bills, putting themselves in perpetual debt. In Montreal's Griffintown, the average weekly wage was less than five dollars.

Low incomes were accompanied by low prices. A Griffintown house could be rented for $6.30 a month and most families took in lodgers at $2 a month. The lower middle class, managers and shopkeepers, could earn $20 a week and paid as much as $16 a month for handsome residences. Eaton's catalogue offered a solid oak bedroom suite for $25. Beef was ten cents a pound, beer five cents a pail, cabbages thirty-five cents a dozen.

whole family worked

Many families managed to scrape by because everyone worked. A labouring man could earn $8 a week, a woman $4.50, a child $3. Although most provinces had enacted some form of compulsory school attendance laws, there was little support for enforcing them. It meant that children worked.

Quebec's Factory Act in 1890 tried to assure that "unhealthy factories" would not hire boys younger than fourteen or girls younger than fifteen; factories designated as both "unhealthy *and* dangerous" were restricted to male employees no younger than sixteen and females no younger than eighteen. A work day for children was supposed to be limited to ten hours.

The Labor Advocate commented admiringly that it was a model piece of legislation which "will remedy some of the most glaring evils of child labour." Six years later Montreal's silk factories, sugar refineries and paint works were still full of children, the taller ones described as adults no matter what their age. Birth records, if they existed at all, could be falsified easily and the penalties for infractions of child labour laws were indulgent. A father in Kingston claimed that all three of his children were born in the same year, making them all eligible for factory work; he was fined a dollar.

Thirteen-year-olds were working sixty-hour weeks in mills; in Cape Breton, mine slits in the coal face too narrow for an adult were worked by twelve-year-old boys. An investigation of the garment industry revealed that children as young as eight working at home sewed buttons all day and into the night. One employer, who regularly had between twenty-five and forty teenage women working for him free, "learning the trade," habitually fired them when the apprentice period was up. A royal commission in 1896 looked at "the sweating system," which it defined as "making clothing under filthy and inhuman conditions." It found children working as late as ten and eleven at night.

Gas irons were used in the clothing factories. Many of them leaked and all of them made closed rooms insufferably hot. An inspector reported that in one loft the steam was so thick the women could not see one another. An employee testified that "even with the improved sewing machines, in ten or eleven years a good able-bodied man will be like a broken-down streetcar horse. It does not take long to break the girls down." The adults died of tuberculosis; it was usually diphtheria that took the children.

piece-work drudgery

Piece-work was not an uncommon method of reducing production costs. In some factories foremen set the piece-work rate at the edge of the employees' endurance and then, when the quota was reached, the foremen would increase the rate. Those who could not meet the increased pressure were fired. There were plenty of jobless waiting for the vacancy. The classic victim of the system was a common sight on the city streets in the nineties, a woman with a face old for her years, bent under the load of an enormous bundle of cloth pieces. The bundles were collected weekly from a sub-contractor and taken home, where a skilled sewer could make a boy's double-breasted coat, with three pockets, half-belt at the back, buttons and button holes for fourteen cents. Often the sub-contractor did not supply the thread, a costly item, and even then the price could be reduced by a

**Herbert Brown Ames
"Watercloset Ames"**

A wealthy Montreal manufacturer and alderman in the '90s, Herbert Brown Ames was one of the few of his class who cared about the poor. He was born in Montreal, educated in the U.S., and influenced by social reformers there. Realizing that lip service and legislation were not enough, he attempted to convince private philanthropists to finance low-cost housing for urban renewal. In his treatise on Montreal's working-class district, *The City Below The Hill,* Ames described the contrast between the poor and wealthy sections of the city and campaigned to rid the city of pollution caused by outhouses. Critics dubbed him "Watercloset Ames" for his trouble, but before he died at age 91, he was knighted and decorated by foreign countries for his pioneer work in health care.

Edmund Sheppard
Saturday Night's **Cowboy**

In many ways he looked like Buffalo Bill – a tobacco chewer with a long drooping moustache and goatee. His days of youth in Mexico and Texas driving stagecoaches and herding cattle had honed a swagger to his gait. Edmund "Don" Sheppard was born in 1855 near St. Thomas, Ont., and educated for the ministry. At 23 he returned from the American "wild west" and worked for several newspapers before taking charge of the Toronto *News,* a sensational piece of yellow journalism printed on pink paper. In 1887 the city's wealthy middle class was ready for its own journal, and Sheppard put out *Saturday Night.* The first issue of 9,500 copies sold out, and by the time Sheppard retired in 1906, the magazine was Canada's most popular weekly. Even its bigoted editorials seemed okay to its 10,000 readers.

"fine" for poor workmanship.

Few Canadians were aware of the conditions in which the overcoats they purchased at their favourite department stores were made. But there were rumours that seamstresses working at home in cold rooms wrapped the coats around sick children and thereby contaminated the cloth.

wage-cutting "fines"

All workers, even those in regular employment, were helpless against wage-cutting "fines" for infractions of rules or production errors, and dangerous working conditions. A union movement was growing though much of it was a reflection of what was happening in the United States. Some 250 locals were organized across Canada during the decade, most of them in Toronto and Montreal. In British Columbia, the Western Federation of Miners got its start in 1895.

The Knights of Labor was behind an 1891 strike in Hull that shut down almost every lumber mill in the Ottawa Valley. The previous year, wages had been cut $1 a week and men working an eleven and a half hour day, six days a week, were drawing between $6 and $8.50 a week. When the workers struck, the millowners cried for help. Four companies of militia were called to break the strike. At the end of the violence one mill agreed to a 10-hour day – hailed as a great victory for the union.

Conditions were even worse elsewhere. Mill workers in Moncton who struck a year earlier had been receiving as little as 54 cents for an 11-hour day. A Toronto union local reported in 1894: "Unemployment is serious among our men . . . 30 per cent of our people are unemployed." One bitterly cold day in February, 1895, jobless men rioted. Hundreds led by black flags on which WORK OR BREAD had been printed, marched on Toronto's City Hall. A wall of police turned them back but

later they tried again. This time they broke through and clambered into the building, where they smashed plaster walls and furniture in the mayor's office.

Newspapers echoed the general opinion that their behaviour was a disgrace. Toronto's *Saturday Night* grumbled that next the poor would be asking for free lemon pies and sponge cake. When coal-handlers in Montreal staged a strike over the hiring of twelve Italian immigrants at lower wages, the *Gazette* reported that "fortunately there was a large posse of police on the scene," adding a sardonic comment on the dirtiness of the strikers, so blackened by coal that the blood drawn by police truncheons hardly showed.

strikers get support

Occasionally the labour movement received some public support. In 1898 streetcar drivers in London, Ontario, members of the Amalgamated Street Railwaymen of North America, struck for better wages and shorter hours. They were receiving 12 cents an hour, and wanted about five cents an hour more. By ten o'clock on the night of October 27, all the streetcars were in the barn. The next day the company attempted to take out car-76 but a crowd of union sympathizers gathered and filled the street blocking the exit. When the strikers met that night at the Princess Rink, five thousand people joined them to wish them well. That weekend, there was a riot, ignited by a striker pulling out a gun. Crowds didn't disperse, even when the Riot Act was read.

Although aware that few jobs existed in the early part of the decade, some white-collar Canadians saw poverty as evidence of poor character. There were few charities or government relief programs and only a scattering of private ones, usually church-sponsored. An organization soliciting donations to buy overcoats and fuel for those in

Potted plants lent an air of respectability to Little Champlain St. in Lower Town, Quebec. Working-class children walked barefoot – but they all wore hats.

The Salvation Army

Fierce opposition greeted Jack Addie and Joe Ludgate when they held their first Salvation Army meeting in London, Ontario, in 1882. Established churches didn't like their brass-band and Christian-soldier brand of evangelism, and they were forced to hold services outdoors or in improvised halls. But the movement spread quickly. In 1890 a small home for wayward women and girls was opened in Toronto, the first in the "Sally Anns'" programme of practical Christianity.

By 1894 the reach of the Salvation Army extended to the B.C. coast, where this group of hastily uniformed Indians rallied around the flag and drum.

need, had to give assurances that a careful investigation would ensure that no able-bodied men received handouts. The country was accustomed to transient tinkers and pedlars. Until mail-order catalogues, rural homemakers depended on such visits for housewares and medicines (and news of the neighbourhood), while city homes relied on street vendors for vegetables, eggs, and fruit. But in the midst of the nineties depression, women went from door to door selling their spoons.

"smiles are rare"

The *Canadian Journal of Medicine and Surgery* reported in 1897, just as economic recovery glimmered, on the number of empty hospital beds, and ascribed it to the unwillingness of anyone to miss a possible day's work. With sensitivity unusual for the era, it noted, "The faces of the people, which to the looker-on are true indices of the colour of their lives, are grave, smiles are rare except where children play."

They played – but in city slums, where a child's life was cruel and often short. It was a common sight to see ragged, stunted children begging in the streets for pennies. The more resourceful among them sold newspapers or shined shoes. These street urchins were considered a nuisance. People complained impatiently but no one had a solution. It was commonly assumed that their parents were drunks or layabouts.

John Kelso was a young police reporter on the Toronto *World*. His job required him to come and go at irregular times and he was alarmed to find midnight streets abounding with shivering children. He was appalled to discover small boys pimping for their sisters.

Two urchins "attired in rags and dirt" came regularly to the *World* office in the middle of the night to beg from reporters and warm themselves by the stove, often falling asleep in exhaustion be-

A Hobo's Alphabet

Hard times in the nineties created a fraternity of hoboes, vagabonds or tramps who roamed the countryside in search of work or a square meal. Shunned by society, these men devised an "alphabet" that rated the hospitality of homes and warned "brothers" of what could be expected down the road: (1) this road is better than the other (2) a good place to rest (3) ferocious dog (4) religious, but charitable (5) good for nothing (6) tired of being charitable (7) may be arrested (8) danger: police (9) doubtful (10) stay awhile (11) be polite (12) have given and will again (13) women alone all day, but armed.

As labour's voice grew stronger in the nineties, agitating for better wages and a shorter work week, a Grip cartoon depicted a business baron's view of hours and wages.

side it. In the courts, Kelso saw children as young as six being sent to prison for theft—an eleven-year-old who had served three years for theft was given another three-year sentence when he stole a lamp; and a nine-year-old prostitute, earning a dime for each customer, was sent off to prison.

Kelso visited orphanages and inquired why such children were not given protection. The response was the children were too dirty and their language offensive. In a mood of frustration and anger, walking into a lashing winter wind late one night he heard children crying. He found a brother and sister huddled in a doorway. They told him their parents would whip them unless they returned with 25 cents; they had been able to beg only 15 cents. It was the final straw for Kelso. He petitioned a court to remove the children from their parents, only to learn there were no laws to protect them. They were sent back home. A short while later they were caught stealing and sent to prison.

horses or children?

A prominent Torontonian wrote indignantly to the *World* suggesting a society for the prevention of cruelty to horses be organized. Donations amounting to $75 arrived at the newspaper, prompting a public meeting. Kelso attended and gave a moving speech about children which persuaded the founding group to extend its concern for horses to include children as well. He quit his job and became the administrator of a shaky new organization, the Humane Society. Later, discouraged that the membership was only peripherally interested in the plight of children, he broke away and founded another group, the Children's Aid Society and Fresh Air Fund.

Kelso's distress at the wretchedness of poverty was shared in Montreal by Herbert Brown Ames, whose outrage took a different tack. In 1887 he

published a book entitled, *The City Below the Hill*, a survey of Montreal's working class. The poor, he wrote, had no plumbing, while the city's well-to-do had indoor toilets and hot and cold water. The city counted almost six thousand outhouses. "It certainly does not seem to me that the work of eradicating this evil is being pushed forward with the energy and despatch which the urgency of the case demands," he wrote. Ames recommended a model of sanitation developed in England known as the Birmingham Pail System, a daily sewage collection service. "Would that Montreal might enter the Twentieth Century with this reform an accomplished fact," he pleaded.

sharp-tongued critic

Open-pit sewage, poor diets, contaminated drinking water, and sweat-shop toil kept life expectancy to a minimum in the slums. Ames noted that in 1893 the death rate in Canada averaged 14 per 1,000, while the death rate in Griffintown was 34 per 1,000.

A new mood was sensed in the country, one of redressing wrongs and championing underdogs. The Methodist Church was advocating social change through its sharp-tongued *Christian Guardian*. Radical clergymen began to interpret Christianity as a gospel of social concern.

William Lyon Mackenzie King, a young university graduate with an interest in reform, wrote four articles in the *Mail and Empire* in 1897 exposing the horrors of the sweating system. The *Labor Advocate*, a weekly endorsed by the Toronto Trades and Labour Council, reported on international labour activities and urged public ownership of utilities. Winnipeg's *Voice* and London's *Industrial Banner* echoed the *Advocate's* editorials.

John Kelso observed with satisfaction, "The world is entering upon an era of social justice." And it was.

Children's World

The child's world in the 1890s was one of strict discipline: long walks to school, strong, stiff clothing fastened by a hundred hooks and eyes, lessons by gaslight, endless Sunday morning sermons, and household chores. But it was a world of simple pleasures, too: a horse-car ride downtown; the smell of Demerara sugar in the cellar, the warmth of the parlour stove, magic lantern slides, sweet buns and ice cream at the confectionary, and the endless folds of Auntie's hoop skirt.

There's a good bit of nostalgia for his farm-boy childhood in George Reid's painting, The Story *(1890). This spell-bound group could be listening to a story of swash-buckling pirates memorized from the popular* Boy's Own Paper.

The poverty in L'Enfant au pain *(1892) was all too familiar to Ozias Leduc, who grew up in the little village of Saint-Hilaire, Quebec.*

When Grandma was a Baby

When grandma was a baby, children were to be seen but not heard. Although attitudes were changing, parents still dressed their kids in miniatures of their own fashion – at least for church and special occasions. Those whose parents could afford them, played with store-bought toys: wax dolls, houses, cooking stoves, wicker prams and tiny tea sets for girls; model stores, railroad trains, steam engines and hobby horses for boys. Blocks, puzzles and games were usual weekday pastimes, replaced on Sundays by Bible games like Proverbs and Noah's Ark. Girls were taught to knit and sew, and on farms to pluck geese and churn butter. Boys were expected to black boots, cut ice and clean "western dirties" – eggs fresh from the market.

Guess who's coming for tea? These two misses better set another place.

Children's fashion of the period was only a slightly modified version of the adult.

The election of 1891 was the Old Chieftain's last hurrah. With his
health failing at age 76, John A. Macdonald campaigned to the point
of exhaustion, orchestrating one final political victory. The issue,
once again, was tariffs and trade relations: the Liberals pressing
for a closer union with the U.S.; the Conservatives raising the
spectre of a Liberal-American plot for an eventual American take-
over. However, coincidence gave the Tories the weapon and advantage
they needed – a set of printer's proofs of a pro-annexation pamphlet
written by Toronto Globe journalist, Edward Farrer. The gambit
worked, and John A. was returned to office with a 27-seat majority.

THE OLD FLAG,
THE OLD POLICY,
THE OLD LEADER.

CHAPTER FOUR

Two Solitudes

*Do they mix with us, assimilate with us,
intermarry with us? Do they read our
literature or learn our laws? No. . . .*

D'Alton McCarthy, 1887

It sometimes appeared that Canada would die of a terminal case of prejudice. Each part of the country seemed to detest and despise every other part; each religion seemed to abhor every other way of expressing faith; English-speaking provinces appeared bent on exterminating the French language. Management would not talk with labour, Grits would not dine with Tories, a divorced person was excommunicated from society, the dries reviled the wets, and vice versa.

"There's no state church in Canada, and the utmost religious liberty prevails," the 1898 *Canada Year Book* assured visitors. But most Canadians believed that a person's religion was a significant indicator of character. Business and social connections were usually formed within the borders of church membership. Anglicans hired Anglicans and sent their children to Anglican schools. Some enterprises were solidly Presbyterian and others, rarely of major significance in the world of finance, were entirely Roman Catholic.

There were benevolent societies, charitable institutions, hospitals and orphanages to serve the sick or needy, but the destitute could appeal for help according to their religion—to the House of

Industry or the National Society, serving only Protestants, or the St. Vincent de Paul Society, which would aid only Roman Catholics. Some reformers realized such separation was foolish and inefficient and recommended instead an integrated system of charity, but nothing was more unlikely in the nineties.

With few exceptions, Canadians in any one part of the country saw themselves as different from Canadians everywhere else, threatened and beleaguered, in great danger unless they kept their dukes up.

The Maritime provinces, for instance, had become so resentful of Confederation that the Nova Scotia government had difficulty mustering a crowd to celebrate Dominion Day. The legislature considered a law to make observance obligatory but it never came to a vote because it was clear it would not pass. Westerners, still raw with the hatreds of the 1885 "rebellion" and the hanging of Riel, wanted little to do with the French or Roman Catholics and were not at all happy with the CPR and Eastern business barons who seemed to be harvesting the profits of their wheat fields like plantation overseers.

The two most wrathful provinces were Manitoba and Quebec. In Manitoba, Protestant homesteaders from Ontario wanted to shut down separate schools; and Quebec witnessed a landslide victory for the nationalist forces headed by Hon-

PRESBYTERIAN DIVINE—"You don't mean to say, my friend, that there are no Christians in these parts?"
NATIVE—"Well, they're durned skarce, it's a fact. Nothin' but Presbyterians along the hull concession line."

A person's religion, language, sex and political party were matters of some importance to most Canadians.

Prejudice

It sometimes seemed that the term "prejudice" didn't exist: Orientals were chinks or coolies; Blacks were coons or niggers; Jews were yids; East Asians were wogs; Catholics were micks; Ukrainians were bohunks; and the French were frogs. If a man was different in language, religion, race or customs, there was a word for him. Canadians weren't the first or worst bigots, of course. Nor were the nineties any different from the decades past. Most people's worlds were still amazingly small, and changes of attitudes slow. After all, Canada was still a cold, god-forsaken place to many Europeans.

"Say, boss, I – I'se afeared I has to leab you heah. Kaint go no furder."

"Why, what's the matter, Mose?"

"Wy, doan you smell dat possum an' sweet taters cookin' up to Pete Smiff's back dar?"

PREPARED.

MINISTER (*to wealthy converted Hebrew on his death bed*) — "Remember, Mr. Goldstein, that a rich man cannot enter the kingdom of heaven."

GOLDSTEIN — "Dot ish all right. I haf put mine broberty in my vife's name."

oré Mercier. English language newspapers were full of the atrocities of the new regime. It was said that Mercier celebrated his political victory in a hall decorated with the flags of France and Quebec, with only one Union Jack in evidence. When a French frigate arrived in harbour at Quebec City, the *fleur de lis* was raised in welcome, with a Union Jack below it. This provoked such a storm in Ottawa and Toronto that an apology had to be made. Quebec said it was "an accident."

Irish feuds break out

It was not particularly helpful in that time of tender feelings that Bishop Laflèche of Trois Rivières, noting that many New England towns were almost totally populated by Quebecois, recommended annexing part of the United States. Horrified Americans rallied to the ancient hate words, "Romanism" and "Papist conspiracy."

Minorities within minorities engaged in sometimes bloody feuds. Irish Catholics in southwestern Ontario fought among themselves – just because they were Irish some thought. The most militant faction in the country was the Equal Rights Association, founded by Orangemen on the proposition of equal rights for everyone, except non-Orangemen. Their leader, D'Alton McCarthy, a brilliant trial lawyer and for some time regarded as the likely successor to John A., stumped the country, speaking as often as three times a day, and always on the theme of limiting French to Quebec. A reporter in southwestern Ontario noted that hats were flung in the air when he cried ringingly that he never wanted to hear another word of French spoken in Canada.

But as Roman Catholics could always vote *en bloc* in Parliament, this defensive juggernaut was enough to defeat an innocuous bill authorizing a charter for an insurance fund: the beneficiaries were to be Orangemen.

The Protestant Protective Association claimed a membership of fifty thousand, whose initiation included a solemn oath never to employ or vote for a Catholic. In 1896 Ottawa's Catholics defeated a municipal plan to build a public library because bishops would not be allowed to censor the books. (There was some justification for Catholic concern as some of the most popular literature of the day dealt with the depravity of nuns and priests.) Methodists and Presbyterians sent missionaries to Quebec to convert the heathen.

Mixed marriages were an abomination, and both Catholic and Protestant parents frightened their children with stories of dark atrocities perpetrated by the other camp. Historian Arthur Lower, born in 1889, recalls that his childhood was tormented by stories of Catholics who would come in the night to slaughter the entire family in their beds. Raised in a civil, educated home in Toronto, Vincent Massey wrote in his memoirs of stories that nuns held children prisoner in the convents. He and other daring boys would peek over the convent wall to watch for captives.

church against church

When the Toronto *Globe*'s editor-in-chief, John Willison, toured the west in 1893, he was fêted by a Catholic host one day and a Protestant on the next. He reported that not once did the hosts speak to one another.

It was news when they did. In 1890 the Montreal *Gazette* commented admiringly on the agreeableness of the French-speaking 65th and some English-speaking regiments who attended a New Year's reception in the armouries together and "set an example to all by being courteous to one another."

For reasons of fair representation, Canada's commissioners at the 1893 World Exposition in Chicago were an Orangeman from Ontario and a

**D'Alton McCarthy
The Crusader**

Even his fellow MP s thought his cross-country crusade for an all-English Canada was rash, if not simple-minded. It embarrassed PM Macdonald and the party and inflamed the feud over the language rights of French-Canadians. He was born in Ireland in 1836, and grew up in Barrie, Ont. A lawyer, he entered politics at age 30 and held a seat in parliament until his death in 1898. Incredible as it seems, John A. once offered him the justice minister's post. McCarthy openly stated his dislike of the French and spouted his views whenever he found an audience. In 1889 he split with the Conservatives and sat as an Independent. His "principles" had been violated, he felt, in the compromises made to the French. He formed what he called the Equal Rights Association to combat the "menace of French domination."

Sir John A. is Dead

"The silver cord is loosed and the great leader is no more," reported the Toronto *Daily Mail*. The grand old man of Canadian politics, John A. Macdonald, died quietly and peacefully at 10:15 P.M., June 6, 1891. He was 76. The country went into mourning, and for a time even Liberals and the recently-elected Tories forgot their past differences.

Thousands of mourners lined Parliament Hill as the cortège passed. In his eulogy, Wilfrid Laurier said: "The life of Sir John A. is the history of Canada."

News headlines summed up his career.

Draped in black satin, the funeral train headed for Kingston, over the track of the CPR John A. had helped to build.

He promised his mother he would be buried at Cataraqui Cemetery. He was – ironically, in an American-made casket.

53

THE **Canadian** MAGAZINE of · Politics · Science · Art · Literature ·

CONTENTS.

The Manitoba Public School Law.
D'ALTON McCARTHY

Anti-National Features of the National
Policy. REV. PRINCIPAL GRANT

The Norsemen the Discoverers of
America. REV. W. S. BLACKSTOCK

Conduct and Manner. PROF. WM. CLARK

In the Shadow of the Arctic. W. W. FOX

Some Modernisms of the Stage.
HECTOR W. CHARLESWORTH

Sir Lancelot. WILLIAM WILFRED CAMPBELL

The Quartier Latin. JOHN HOME CAMERON

The Regenerators. UNCLE THOMAS

An Open Window, and What
Came of It. WILLIAM T. JAMES

The Birds' Lullaby. E. PAULINE JOHNSON

"Which Is It?" EDWARD J. TOKER

In Imitation of Horace. S. P. MORSE

$2.50 PER ANNUM.   SINGLE COPIES, 25 CENTS.

MARCH 1893.   ONTARIO PUBLISHING CO LTD, TORONTO

Topping the list of well-known writers in this 1893 issue of the Canadian Magazine *is an article on the Manitoba school controversy by D'Alton McCarthy.*

Catholic from Quebec. Neither could overcome the barrier of mutual detestation. They refused to speak to each other and the exhibit was a disaster.

When John A. died in office in 1891, the issue of religion permeated all discussion of his successor. The compromise candidate was a Protestant, an ailing man of limited talents, John Abbott. He could tolerate the intrigues and spite for only a year. "If it were not for the deputations wanting money and lands, and the people wanting situation and plunder, I should get on pretty well," he grumbled before quitting.

receive hate mail

The ablest man found in the party was John Thompson, minister of justice and a former judge of Nova Scotia's Supreme Court. Thompson, however, was a Methodist who had converted to Catholicism, which made him seem doubly-damned by Protestants and a touch suspicious to Catholics.

Thompson's appointment as Prime Minister was fought most fiercely by Orangeman McCarthy, who threatened to resign his seat in Parliament. The threat died amidst a storm of invective. Protestants who accepted posts in Thompson's cabinet received hate mail including accusations that they were dupes of the Jesuits. Protestants were mollified somewhat when Thompson appointed Clarke Wallace to a key patronage position, Controller of Customs. Wallace was a founder of the Equal Rights Association and Grand Master of the Orange Order of British North America.

Thompson went to England in 1894 to visit Queen Victoria and abruptly died of a heart attack during a state luncheon. The desperate Conservatives looked along the thinning front bench and this time picked as leader and prime minister a weak, fussy, 75-year-old Orangeman, Mackenzie Bowell. He kept the office warm while the Tories persuaded Charles Tupper to leave his post of Canadian High Commissioner in London and come home to lead them into an election.

Meanwhile, events exacerbated in the West. The North-West Territories, encompassing yet-to-be-formed Saskatchewan and Alberta, already had abolished French language rights. Manitoba's Catholic majority had easily secured protection for the language in 1870 and in 1888 the provincial premiership was won by Grit Protestant, Thomas Greenway after his alliance with the French.

Just two years later, however, Protestant homesteaders from Ontario were a majority in the province and helped Manitoba legislate, at least tentatively, against Catholic schools and the French language. French-speaking Manitobans demanded that the federal government do something about the legislation, though no one knew for certain if it could. The basic question was whether taxes could be used to support the province's separate school system. According to the British North America Act, which had not anticipated such a dilemma, schools were a provincial affair. The matter went to the Supreme Court of Canada, which declared that Manitoba had violated the Constitution. The nation teetered, extremists thought, with the future of provincial rights and unity in the balance.

Catholics were aghast

The case was appealed to England's Privy Council Judicial Committee which reversed the Supreme Court of Canada decision. Manitoba Catholics, aghast, pressed for another hearing. Eighteen months later came the same ruling—provinces could discard language rights if they pleased. The Judicial Committee added however that an aggrieved minority could ask Ottawa for help.

The election of 1896 was fought mainly on the issue—even the tariff question became secondary.

It was Charles Tupper's Tories against the Liberal's choice, Wilfrid Laurier. During the five days and nights of savage parliamentary debate over the Manitoba school question that preceded the election, Laurier threw Quebec into an uproar by defending the rights of provinces, and added that the churches, both Protestant and Catholic, should stay out of politics. It was an extraordinary stand in such a time. Both the Liberals and Conservatives had inner schisms along religious lines to the degree that the Prime Minister did not dare call a caucus. French-Canadian nationalists and church officials were drumming up solid support for federal action against Manitoba, while Protestant ministers remained passionately against federal intervention. Laurier's speech in March, 1896, rose serene and sensible over the tumult:

Laurier called a traitor

I am here acknowledged leader of a government party, composed of Roman Catholics and Protestants as well, as Protestants must be in the majority in every party in Canada . . . So long as I have a seat in the House, so long as I occupy the position I do now, whenever it shall become my duty to take a stand upon any question whatsoever, that stand I will take not upon grounds of Catholicism, not upon grounds of Protestantism, but upon grounds which can appeal to the conscience of all men, irrespective of their particular faith, upon grounds which can be occupied by all men who love justice, freedom and toleration.

It was a stand that some thought would likely destroy his Quebec support. He was called a traitor, and worse. Childhood friends cut him dead and there were dark stories of payoffs by Protestants. It did not improve his credibility within his home province when he visited Toronto a few weeks later and was accorded an ovation. Leading citizens, Protestants all, unhitched his horses and per-

It was a great day for Belleville, Ontario, when former printer and publisher Mackenzie Bowell came home as prime minister of Canada in 1894. He was 71 at the time.

Montreal Star artist Henri Julien depicted PM Wilfrid Laurier as an accomplished song-and-dance man after his 1896 election victory.

sonally pulled his carriage through the streets, the era's equivalent to a ticker tape parade, while citizens lined the curbs and cheered.

Some priests told their flock they would be committing a mortal sin if they voted for Laurier. Catholic bishops drew up an inflammatory document aimed at Laurier, which was returned only when Toronto's Bishop Walsh refused to sign it. A collective pastoral was issued on May 16 which ordered that "all Catholics should vote only for candidates who will formally and solemnly pledge themselves to vote in Parliament in favour of the legislation giving to the Catholics of Manitoba the school laws which are recognized as theirs . . . " Bishop Lafleche of Trois Rivières declared that a Catholic who voted for Laurier would be "sinning in a grave manner."

Bishop Emard of Valleyfield remained neutral, a valiant position in that cauldron. Israel Tarte, the renegade Conservative out of favour for his zeal in exposing Tory corruption, worked tirelessly for Laurier. J.-F. Guité, Liberal candidate in Bonaventure, was asked to promise he would vote against Laurier's compromise on the Manitoba school question if elected. In an echo of Edmund Burke's renowned speech at Bristol, Guité declared, "In all public questions I claim the freedom enjoyed by every British subject . . . I cannot before God and my conscience renounce the freedom of exercising my privilege as Member to the best of my judgement."

Despite the efforts of the clergy and despite appeals to old prejudices, Quebec voted for the Grits and Laurier, the province's first native-son premier of Canada. Guité was also elected, with a three-to-one majority.

Laurier's policy of "the sunny way," a peculiarly Canadian blend of compromise and massive inactivity, was achieved. Manitoba was required to provide bilingual instruction wherever more than ten children spoke a language other than English, which was practically impossible since the province was a rich mixture of Jews, Icelanders and eastern and middle Europeans. But it served to defuse the tension.

A curious trade-off took place in the background of the conflict between Quebec's clergy and the Liberals. In the end, with some influence from Rome, the Catholic hierarchy was persuaded to temper the "Holy War" that was developing over Manitoba while Liberals yielded on an issue which had long been dear to them, the freeing of the schools from clerical domination. Liberalism had been resurrected in Quebec.

Prime Minister for a Day

John Joseph Caldwell Abbott

When John A. Macdonald died the Conservative Party looked along their parliamentary bench for a replacement and came up with a compromise candidate in John Abbott. He was a brilliant lawyer, former head of McGill's law school. In 1873 he had been implicated in the Pacific Scandals by evidence made public by one of his own clerks, but he had learned his lesson. He had been appointed to the Senate in 1887, and when the PM's chair became vacant, he reluctantly agreed to fill the position. He hated politics and loved to play whist and cribbage. "I hate notoriety, public meetings, public speeches, caucuses . . ." As PM his first concern was to clean up a patronage scandal within his cabinet. But the job was too much for him. His health failing, he resigned in 1892 and died at 72.

John Sparrow David Thompson

Parliamentary pundits all agreed that John A.'s logical successor should have been a younger man – John Thompson of Nova Scotia. Macdonald had called him "the greatest discovery of my life," but that wasn't blessing enough. Thompson was a convert to Roman Catholicism – a "pervert" in the Protestant vernacular. To avoid causing further fissures in the party, Thompson declined. When Abbott resigned, there was no other choice. He was a capable man with good common sense and a careful eye for private and public money, rare among politicians of the day. Much of his term he spent in trade talks and the legal wrangle over the issue of Manitoba's separate schools. His doctors advised he take a rest in 1894, and he went to England. At lunch at Windsor Castle he died of a heart attack.

Mackenzie Bowell

Thompson's untimely death threw the Tories into another frenzy. The logical choice was Charles Tupper, but Lady Aberdeen, the governor general's wife, disliked the man, and urged her husband to appoint anyone but Tupper. Mackenzie Bowell was 71, an MP for 35 years and a staunch anti-Catholic. Thompson had shuffled him off to the Senate in 1892, but he was recalled. A party divided over the separate school issue greeted him. The cabinet proposed a bill to woo back the French and Catholic vote, but Bowell refused to act on it. A year later, the party steadily losing support and Bowell still sitting on the fence, half his cabinet walked out – "a nest of traitors," Bowell called them. In April 1896, Charles Tupper was recalled from England and Bowell's days as PM were ended.

Charles Tupper

He was 75 years old when the title passed on to him, and for once there was little argument. In his own account of affairs, Charles Tupper said: "When I came to Canada last winter, I found the Conservative party utterly demoralized . . ." He had been a politician for over 40 years, trained as a doctor in his youth in Nova Scotia before entering politics. He had been one of the motive forces in the Maritimes in Confederation days and had held several positions in all levels of government. In 1896, however, despite his best efforts, time had run out for his party, and his term lasted six months. A new breed of politician was waiting in the wings, this time a French-Canadian, and a Catholic, one who didn't smoke, drink or play politics for money. The era of John A. was over, too.

CHAPTER FIVE

The Railway Comes to Come-By-Chance

It seems that the Ministry are going to sell the colony to a contractor . . . a rather novel proceeding.

Joseph Chamberlain, colonial secretary, 1898

If the Canadian Pacific Railway in its second decade was the adhesive strip holding Confederation together, the railways criss-crossing the Maritimes were also serving the national purposes. Long the provinces of wood, wind and water, resources which by the nineties were showing ever-diminishing returns, the Maritimes had begun to realize that the bounty of coal and ore beneath their feet just might fuel their way to a brighter economic future.

No national dream spurred the builders of the Atlantic lines. The time-honoured system of patronage and subsidies levelled the roadbeds and fired the engines of the old 561-mile Intercolonial, linking Halifax and Rivière du Loup, but its cargo – coal from the Nova Scotia deposits – was finding an easy market on the Atlantic and along the St. Lawrence. In 1887 the Eastern Extension Railway stretched its terminus to New Glasgow on Cape Breton Island, and for the first time the region's century-old mining industry was able to look forward to year-round transportation of its coal, no longer hampered by the winter freeze-up in the Gulf of St. Lawrence.

In the nineties Newfoundland attempted for the second time to build a railway from St. John's to the copper, coal and lead deposits on the west coast. The first attempt at a railway had come in the seventies when Newfoundlanders, desperate to end their total dependence on the sea, first discovered the Island's mineral potential. Sandford Fleming himself had surveyed the route from the capital due west through virgin forests, across territory unimportant to a people who kept their eyes to the sea.

The terminus was to be St. George's Bay, some five hundred miles from St. John's, but only the first spike had been driven when word came from England to stop at once. France had complained about the potential disruption of her fishing territory and England, which had given France one third of the colony's far coastline in 1713, stood loyal to the old commitment to French fishing rights. Work on the railway stopped.

Britain had been consistent in its 300-year-old relationship with the Empire's first colony. Her attitude of baleful indifference to the island's well-being never wavered. In 1875 when geologists found lead ore at Port-au-Port on the French shore, a protest from Paris to the colonial office in London resulted in an order to close the mine.

Newfoundlanders noted a few years later that France had west coast rights to all species of fish, but the old agreement made no mention of lobster. By 1889 there were sixty lobster canning factories

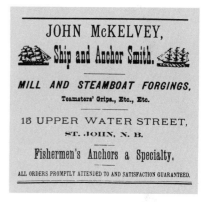

Maritimers and Newfoundlanders traditionally looked to the sea for their livelihood and depended on shipsmiths like John McKelvey.

Opposite page: *Downtown St. John's lies in ruins after the great fire of 1892. Looking west down Water St. (left) and Gower St. (centre), only skeletons of brick were left of the city built entirely of wood.*

A Newfoundland sealer stands on an ice washed deck, harpoon in hand, beard frozen with sea spray. For men like this, the seal hunt off the northern coast was a major source of income.

along the coast. When France asked Britain to shut them down, it was discovered that treaties covering fisheries had been allowed to expire fifty-six years earlier. It was awkward for the colonial office, but true to form, Newfoundlanders were instructed to close the lobster factories until the matter was straightened out, at a loss of £40,000 a year revenue.

A *Daily Mail* correspondent from London wrote scathingly in 1897, "Profits still, in the main, find their way to the Old Country – the funds of the local capitalists go to England or the United States. The colony was sucked dry." Isaac Morris, a Newfoundland clergyman, added bitterly, "the wonder is, that we are a people at all."

Newfoundland abandoned

Newfoundland indeed bore the look of an abandoned orphan. The outports were full of deserted homes, the occupants gone to look in British Columbia, Manitoba, the States, or St. John's for jobs. The Reverend Morris, touring the coast, lecturing in school-halls on the evils of drink on behalf of the Citizen's Temperance Association of St. John's, observed, "Many of them would prefer staying in their own land, could they make a living."

The entire population depended one way or another on the spring seal hunt and on cod, salmon and lobster fishing. In 1890 the island finally established a Fisheries Department to regulate the industry and cultivate cod and lobster. Business was brisk – during Lent, Catholic countries bought $3,000,000 worth of Newfoundland cod – but little of the money seemed to filter down to the man in the dory. A fresh catch, green cod that wasn't salted or cured, sold for a dollar a hundredweight. If the fisherman could wait to salt or cure the fish, the price was four dollars a hundredweight, but few could afford the delay. They lived

Sydney, Nova Scotia's Dominion Coal company office workers, including three "typewriters," were kept busy with the firm's Atlantic mining operations.

The Dancing Master

In 1866 a strange man arrived in St. John's, Nfld., with the calling card *Charles Henry Danielle – Costumier and Dancing Master*. The city had little use for his refined talents, and when fire destroyed one of his pavilions, he vanished. In 1888 he reappeared, setting up extravagant and unusual dining and dancing establishments like the Octagon Castle (below). The place was an eccentric's delight, decorated to excess with satin, lace and velvet of every possible colour. Single meals were 50¢ and "married meals" $1. The "Professor" was an expert at needlework, and kept his hand-embroidered coffin on display in the castle's mortuary room.

their lives in debt, borrowing every year against their catch.

The catch in 1888-89 was poor. French cod prices undercut Newfoundland's catch on world markets and outport fishermen mounted sporadic attempts to retaliate by refusing to sell the French herring for bait.

centuries of poverty

After centuries of poverty, a sense of hope came to Newfoundland in the nineties. The island's entire revenue from customs duties and exports amounted to a paltry $1,564,457 in 1895. But geologists had discovered minerals, a stubborn agricultural area was producing crops, and there were beginnings in manufacturing. Saw mills were now producing lumber which Newfoundland, with vast tracts of timber in her midst, had previously *imported*.

The trans-Newfoundland railway, started in 1881 and financed through land grants, ran north to farmland and mines, and by 1888 had reached Harbour Grace and Placentia. However, the railway that Newfoundlanders believed would make the country solvent, the one that France had blocked, would run west parallel to the French coast and connect St. John's with mining towns and by boat with the mainland.

Robert Reid, a Scottish financier from Montreal, unaffected by the Island's difficulties, arrived in St. John's with an offer the impoverished administration could not refuse. He would build a 548 mile railway to Port aux Basques, linking St. John's to a jetty pointed at Cape Breton, in return for 2,500,000 acres of Newfoundland's interior. Few Newfoundlanders cared about the interior anyway, which was appraised at about thirty cents an acre. The offer was accepted. As reporter Beckles Willson noted, it was the island's only chance: "Local capital is rarely invested here."

Construction began in 1892 with as much secrecy as could be maintained under the circumstances. William Vallance Whiteway, Newfoundland's premier, explained, "We hesitated about giving away any information whatever as to what we were doing until we had the road and the jetty constructed, lest the French would protest."

The isolation of some outport communities had bred superstitions in Conception Bay that steam locomotives were destructive demons. An irate mob drove surveyors and engineers off the site. As the angry crowd grew to over five hundred, police were summoned to hold them back. The confrontation lasted for five days before residents were persuaded to accept the railway.

Before the railway was completed, however, two major disasters befell the optimistic Islanders. In 1892 St. John's was destroyed in a holocaust swept before the wind that funnels constantly through its steep-sided harbour. The fire destroyed almost three-quarters of the town, and property damage was estimated at $20,000,000, most of it not covered by insurance.

the worst disaster

Isaac Morris wrote, "The fire swept away treasures of a lifetime, and the landmarks of generations, and laid in ruins our principle buildings." St. John's had been burned to the ground before, in 1816 and again in 1846, but this was the worst disaster of all. The Anglican cathedral was caught in the blaze, only its stone walls left standing. The Athenaeum, a cultural centre which included a library, meeting rooms and a music and lecture hall, was reduced to rubble.

Homeless Newfoundlanders stoically rebuilt their houses and businesses. Streets were laid out again, this time wider than they had been, though the Islanders still preferred their doors tight to the sidewalk rather than set back.

There was serious talk behind closed doors in St. John's two years later in 1894. The colony's debt stood at $16 million. The Imperial government had refused to extend any further loans without a prior commission of inquiry into all aspects of government and finance – public officials were alleged to have their hands deep in the people's purse.

On December 10, the Island's only two banks, the Union and the Commercial in St. John's, closed their doors. Their collapse was followed by a run on the government's Newfoundland Savings Bank and it too suspended operations. The island was left without currency. Factories closed because there was no money to pay salaries and stores closed because there were no customers.

started at the top

Premier Whiteway had few options: he could push for confederation with Canada; sell the right to responsible government for England's financial assistance; or try to procure a loan from some other source. As crafty a politician as ever there was, he decided to start at the top of his list.

The overwhelming majority of the Island's 210,000 inhabitants were adamantly opposed to union with Canada, as Whiteway knew, but he approached Mackenzie Bowell, then prime minister of Canada, anyway. Whiteway told him Newfoundland would join Canada if Ottawa would assume the public debt. It was a good investment, he maintained. The Island's fisheries *alone* produced an average of $6 million each year and the mineral riches of Bell Island were only beginning to be tapped.

But 1894 was a lean year for all of Canada. Bowell offered ten million for Newfoundland. Whiteway declined indignantly. He felt privately, and said so later, that Charles Tupper would not have haggled. He pointed out to Bowell that Canada

Henry Beckles Willson
The Tenth Islander

First of all, Beckles Willson was not a Newfoundlander. He was a young journalist, Montreal-born and Kingston-educated. In 1897, when he published the first of his 26 books, *The Tenth Island*, many of the big-wigs of St. John's were outraged. How dare this mainlander publish "some account of Newfoundland, its people, its politics, its problems, and its peculiarities!" But Willson was a crack-reporter, and he hit a few of the sources of the Island's problems in the '90s on the head when he singled out the government's railway policies for criticism. Like Newfoundland's crises, Willson blew over, but he didn't quit his brand of investigative writing. In 1911 he wrote a work titled, *Nova Scotia, the province that has been passed by*.

**Wilfred Grenfell
A Labrador Doctor**

In 1892 an Oxford-trained doctor toured Labrador for the Mission to Deep-Sea Fishermen. The poverty, disease and lack of medical care he found moved Wilfred Grenfell to dedicate his life to improving the condition. He established a medical mission, set up schools, hospitals and nursing stations, and fought for co-operative stores to replace the traditional system of "trucking" – a bartering scheme that kept the fishermen forever in debt. He financed his work through book sales (he wrote 20), lectures and fund-raising trips. Critics, of course, called him a self-promoter. In 1912 he opened a seamen's hostel in St. John's, hoping to provide an alternative to Water St. bars. Before his death in 1940, he was knighted, and honoured by world medical and geographical groups.

had been willing to pay for a railway as the price for getting British Columbia into Confederation, and should be willing to do the same for Newfoundland since most of the Island's public debt was the result of railway building. Bowell was not impressed. Ten million was his best offer. Whiteway, disgusted, refused.

Union with Canada, of sorts, was already taking place while the men negotiated. Within days of Black Monday, three Canadian banks established branches in St. John's – the Bank of Montreal, the Bank of Nova Scotia, and the Merchants' Bank of Halifax. They moved into deserted shops on Water Street, put rough OPEN FOR BUSINESS signs in the windows, and welcomed customers.

Whiteway turned to Britain for emergency help and was able to secure a loan of $3 million. The rest was raised in Montreal and New York by Newfoundland businessmen, led by Robert Bond.

Robert Reid, meanwhile, acquired more and more of the island as a reward for building the railway. When Newfoundland's banks collapsed he pressed for even more concessions. The helpless government proceeded to turn over not only more land, but control of the railway, shipping lines, the telegraph, mineral and timber rights, and the St. John's drydock.

pained by the criticism

Premier Whiteway was pained by the criticism he had to endure as a result. "Defamatory telegrams and newspaper articles" were giving Newfoundland a bad name abroad, he said, and "inhabitants who rushed to the press to air their crude ideas and express decided opinions upon the subject on which they know nothing" were setting back progress.

The opposition press, two St. John's papers, the *Daily News* and the *Herald*, demonstrated a flair for invective. Beckles Willson commented that he

had never seen such "delicious blackguardism" in his entire career. "The Whiteway party is a shameless gang of boodlers, rogues and jobbers," he declared. "The citizens are sick of them and their ringleaders."

full of bustle

Four years after the collapse of the banks and five years after the fire, St. John's once again appeared full of bustle and Newfoundland quirkiness. Willson, the reporter, was delighted to observe that men who loitered around the provincial buildings for political handouts called the premier "skipper" and spat tobacco expertly on the Ionic porticos. The stores didn't look like much on the outside, and employed some casual inventory techniques – "slippers are mysteriously dragged out of biscuit boxes, and barrels conspicuously labelled flour are found, upon inspection, and often to the obvious astonishment of the clerk, to contain corsets" – but these descendants of English merchants were turning over as much as three million dollars a year in 1897.

The fire department was reorganized and the town divided into three fire districts. The firehalls were the last word in ingenuity. Harnesses were suspended over each horse's stall, to be dropped on their neck when the bell sounded. The firemen were trained by the clock: they could be dressed and on the rigs in forty seconds. The whole department, consisting of 124 men, thirteen horses, forty-five alarm boxes and three steam engines, cost St. John's $9,000 a year but was worth every cent. It was said, with pride, to be the best fire department in the world, capable of reaching the scene of a fire anywhere in the city within four minutes.

Immigration had almost ceased and Newfoundlanders, often inter-related, evinced a lively interest in one another's activities. An 1897 advertisement in the *Daily News* read: "As a large number of people in the city are given to gossip concerning my actions and personal affairs, I hereby give notice that on and after this date I intend lying on my right side instead of my left as heretofore. (signed) Reuben Wall."

The railway was completed in 1898, one year after the island celebrated the 400th anniversary of John Cabot's visit. The coaches combined English and American influences, containing first and second class compartments in long cars where tea was served, steeped seven times and boiled a few hours the way Newfoundlanders liked it. At the end of the line was the *S.S. Bruce*, a jaunty passenger steamer, armoured against ice, that sailed three times a week for Cape Breton at a respectable clip of fifteen knots.

As the Islanders looked back over the decade, the accomplishments and the setbacks, they soon realized what a heavy price they had paid.

A people who in 1889 had thrown out the government over the disappearance of a carpet following a dance in the Assembly Room, were not long in dealing with Robert Reid's acquisition of most of Newfoundland. In 1901 Newfoundland paid Reid $2,500,000 and bought back some of itself.

an end to poverty?

Reid, however, was but the most conspicuous example of a process that was well underway in the nineties. Mineral discoveries brought in a wave of foreign investors, who were speedily followed by more. There was Canadian money in the iron deposits on Bell Island, and English money in the newsprint manufactured at Grand Falls, a company which acquired power rights on the Exploits River and 7,400 square miles of timberland.

Whatever the price, the citizens of Newfoundland were delighted to have the foreign capital. It appeared that three hundred years of poverty was at last coming to an end.

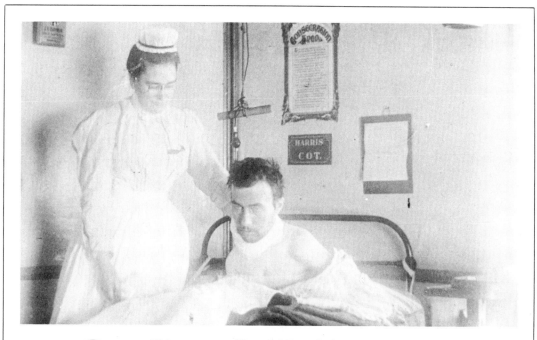

Dr. Grenfell's Mission

Wilfred Grenfell's parish was the sea, the tiny coastal outports and shacks that dotted the Labrador shore. Fishermen had eked out an existence here for over two centuries. The first missions had been built in the 1770s by Moravian Brethren, an evangelical sect, but despite their best efforts, disease and poverty were the common lot. In 1892 Dr. Grenfell established his first medical mission, hired trained nurses (above) and worked with the Moravians (below).

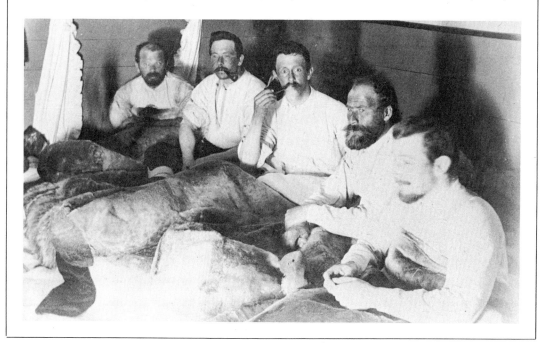

The Mode in Costume

The '90s was a period of change, and nowhere was this more apparent than women's fashion. The bustle was finally gone (thank heavens!), but couturiers were far from ready to let the natural figure show itself. The tight-laced corset remained the foundation of the look of the era – the wasp waist. Skirts and dresses were tight at the hips and flared to the ground in a bell shape. Petticoats were all frills and lace in a rainbow of colours, and coquettish young women showed these (and an inch of stocking!) with a studied gesture when crossing streets. Sleeves grew out of all proportion, from the modest leg-of-mutton puff to the enormous balloon of mid-decade. Women's sportswear copied men's styles of the day in hats, jackets, ties and blouses called "shirtwaisters." As cycling became the obsession, baggy divided skirts called "bloomers" reappeared (they had first been seen in the 1860s) and stirred up a great fuss, denounced in the press and from many pulpits. Men's fashion did not change much: the frock or morning coat, worn with peg-top trousers, was still *de rigueur,* but younger men took to wearing shorter jackets for informal occasions. The clean-shaven look was well-established, although neatly cropped moustaches and beards gave a gentleman an air of distinction and maturity.

D.8. D.9.

Visiting Toilettes.

The Delineator.   DESCRIBED ON PAGE 140.   February, 1898.

Two visiting toilettes from 1898 feature the long, slim, tight-fitting sleeve.

The tight-waist style of the '90s seems exaggerated by the balloon sleeve of '96.

SINGLE-BREASTED FALL OVERCOAT
FLY FRONT,
PREVAILING SHADES.

MEN'S CASSIMERE SACK SUIT.

The style for 1893, by T&D of Stratford and Guelph, Ont.

MEN'S BLACK WORSTED CUTAWAY
COAT AND VEST

BOY'S ULSTER

THE LORD ABERDEEN

The boys' sack suit (right) took the governor general's name.

1869

Boneshaker – wood spokes, steel-rimmed wheels.

1876

Safety Bicycle – introducing rear-wheel drive.

1884

Ladies' Safety Bicycle – with chain drive.

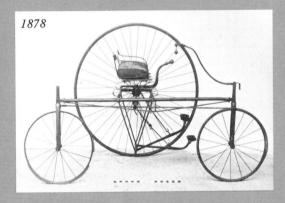

1878

Coventry Tricycle – what'll they think of next?

1885

Rover Bicycle – modern except for solid tires.

1886

Cross-Frame – hints of the trapezoidal frame.

1869

Phantom – the first wire spokes in tension.

1884

Ordinary Bicycle – the legendary racer.

1893

Bantam – the pneumatic tire makes its debut.

CHAPTER SIX

Penny~Farthings, Boneshakers and Silver~Singers

The number of bicycles in Edmonton this season is very large . . . and increasing. That they frighten horses is unquestionable.

Edmonton Bulletin, 1895

A Canadian didn't have to be very old—twenty would do—to believe that he or she lived in the most splendid age of discovery the world had ever known. Well-to-do households had telephones, central heating, indoor toilets, electric light.

Manitobans were raising cattle and holding them in check with new fences of barbed wire. Stores had cash registers and offices had typewriters. Newspapers were installing linotype machines, clattering behemoths splashing liquid lead that cooled like jewels on raw wooden floors. The Masseys were making marvellous farm machinery admired the world over. Their self-binding harvester was becoming a fixture on the prairie landscape. In 1895 Colonel John Moodie took a motorboat, the first in Canada, for a spin on Hamilton Bay.

Improvements to gramophones being manufactured by the "big three"—Berliner, Thomas Edison and Victor—were made at such a pace that sometimes the matter of securing a patent was overlooked. In 1897, Emile Berliner applied for a Canadian patent and set up a factory in Montreal to produce not only gramophones but cylinder records. One of his young employees, Joe Jones, was working on something new that year, a wax record, flat as a platter, on which grooves were engraved. Columbia bought Jones' patent for $25,000. As it turned out, it wasn't much of a bargain since Jones, strictly speaking, didn't have exclusive rights to the idea.

A Berliner advertisement of the day in *Canadian Magazine* promised that the gramophone "will cause more happiness in the household than any other Christmas gift, because it will entertain and amuse every member of the family—from grandmother down to baby." It cost $7.50 for the small one, $15 for the big one. Both came with three free records and were guaranteed for five years.

The gramophone was only the beginning. Thomas Ahearne and Warren Soper of Ottawa demonstrated a new kitchen wonder in 1891, an electric stove. That year the railway tunnel under the St. Clair River was opened, connecting Canada and the United States.

The CPR looked elsewhere and bought steamships, the *Empress of India*, the *Empress of Japan*, and the *Empress of China*. Canadian investors were leaping into Latin America and the Caribbean. William Van Horne, James Ross, Donald Mann, Alexander Mackenzie and William Mackenzie (not related) were making fortunes. The two Mackenzies had been part of a group called the Sao Paulo Light and Power Company. William is known to have said, "I haven't been to Sao Paulo

A championship team of double trick cyclists headlined this show of the Belleville Rambler's Wheel Club. Cycle clubs across the country held exhibitions, races and "rambling" excursions during their heyday.

Ad men had a field day in the '90s when bicycle mania hit the streets. Stearn's riders cycled out of the sunset of the old century into the new; dealers called competitors' lines "primeval and antedeluvian," touting their own wares as "perfect in every detail," "20th-century ideas," "up-to-date," etc. etc. etc.

but I've taken a million dollars out of there in the past three years." And Van Horne, who built a railway in Guatemala that improved life for the United Fruit Company, commented on that experience: "We asked for everything we could think of and we got all we asked for."

new natural resources

Canada, once dependent on beaver, cod and timber, was discovering new natural resources. Prairie wheat might have been one of them but the best variety, Red Fife, ripened too slowly and was often picked off by early frost. Will Saunders, a feisty, egocentric pioneer wheat breeder, had some early ripening hybrid strains growing at the government experimental farm at Brandon in 1892. The breeds were a long way from development and proof that any of them would be high-yielding and high-quality, but Saunders was already working with his son on perfecting the strain.

That year the Edmonton *Bulletin* reported that there were traces of oil in Alberta. Silver was struck at Kimberley, B.C. and gold discovered in the Klondike in 1896.

Working alone, Thomas Ahearne of Ottawa developed a heating system for streetcars and a sweeper to remove snow from tracks and switchpoints. Thomas L. Willson, who discovered carbide and acetylene gas, started his own gas works at Merritton, Ontario, also in 1892. The Allan brothers, whose steamships crossed the Atlantic on fixed schedules as reliable as Yankee clocks, established the Allan Steamship Company in Montreal and their passenger ships ruled the waves. And Newfoundland had a railroad from one end to the other, the bumpiest, proudest ride anywhere.

There was more coming. In Germany, Gottleib Daimler had invented a horseless carriage in 1885 powered by an internal combustion engine. The horseless carriage was being imitated in backyard sheds all across the country by young men with mechanical savvy and grand dreams. The Dixon Carriage Works in Toronto produced the first Canadian motor car in 1893, and that year F.B. Fetherstonhaugh was a sight to see on the streets of Toronto, among the carriages and streetcars, driving an electric car at the dazzling speed of fifteen miles an hour.

Five years later, the intrepid Col. John Moodie of Hamilton gained the debateable distinction of being Canada's first motorist when he purchased a Winton automobile in the United States on April 6, 1898. The Winton people said it was the second automobile sold in North America, the first Winton having been sold to an American the previous day. Col. Moodie paid $1,000 for the car, which he claimed was cheaper to own than a pair of good horses.

Meanwhile, Alexander Graham Bell was testing kites and heavier-than-air flying machines at his Cape Breton summer home, thoughtfully teaching himself aerodynamics.

bicycle academies launched

No invention – no miracle common cold cure or new-fangled widgit – had such an overall impact on the nineties as the mass production of *comfortable* bicycles. "Whoever invented the bicycle deserves the thanks of humanity," declared a British statesman. But there wasn't a high-hearted young man in Europe or North America who didn't know the genealogy of the bicycle backwards. Newspapers began to refer to "the age of the bicycle," and *Scientific American* declared that the bicycle would change the history of the world.

People, especially young people, went daffy and delirious over bicycles. Communities bristled with bicycle sheds, bicycle academies, bicycle shops. Delegations of bicycle enthusiasts were besieging civic fathers to finally pave the roads.

There were local bicycle clubs and national bicycle clubs, issuing maps marked with the location of inns springing up to serve bicycling tourists. Annual bicycle shows introducing new models and accessories were packed to the doors. A minister in the Klondike visited his various gold mining parishes on his bicycle.

front-wheel cranks

Bicycles had been almost a century in the making. In the early 1800s Europeans amused themselves with hobby horses on wheels, a sort of walker propelled by the rider's feet on the ground. In 1855 a French boy of fourteen, Ernest Michaux, was repairing a foot-powered bicycle when he hit on the notion of putting cranks on the front wheel.

Michaux's invention was called a velocipede but its owners promptly gave it another name, the bone-shaker. Its wooden wheels and solid iron frame did precious little to cushion the shock of cobblestone streets and pitted dirt lanes, afflicting the rider with an all-over vibrato. Still, the independence it provided made it a hit and there were velocipede academies in every town and velocipede races attracted multitudes.

To protect the wooden wheel, blacksmith Pierre Lallemont sheathed it in iron in 1865. He also designed a velocipede with a front wheel larger than the back, a ratio that added speed. His contraption weighed more than a hundred pounds but improvements followed rapidly. Innovators lightened it with frames of hollow steel and thin metal spokes instead of wood. A humanitarian attached a rubber cushion to the wheel.

With the weight reduced to about fifty pounds, the frenzy for speed resulted in a grotesque enlargement of the front wheel to more than five feet in diameter. The rider of the quivering, tippy "penny-farthings" sat perilously high off the ground and had to mount from a convenient

Bicycle shops scrambled for sales rights to new lines. Griffiths' claimed to be the world's largest dealers; Walker's featured ladies' wheels and outfits showing the new "bishop" sleeve.

This sporty Vancouver quintet takes a breather at a Stanley Park hollow tree.

The faces are so familiar . . . didn't we just see you at the hollow tree? (left)

"You hold my handlebar, I'll hold yours, and . . . steady now." This "well-balanced" Ottawa group has cycled to Dr. Niall's cottage in Aylmer for the day.

Taking to the Road

Tighten the bow on your bonnet, and *do* straighten your tie – after all, it is Sunday. If Jack hasn't forgotten the map again, and we don't have to rely on those farmers' devilish directions, we should reach the inn before mid-day. Quite a little set-to there last weekend with those horse-men! Well, their days are numbered. It's going to be a pleasant tour, if the other forty in the club can keep up with us for twenty miles. Mustn't forget the puncture kit and tools: a few bad roughs on the road. And keep an eye on that young couple over there. How they do carry on . . . and not even properly engaged.

No casualties in this pile-up; just a few lads from Vancouver on a Sunday pedal, wondering which wheel is whose, and if anyone knows the way back into town.

Bicycle Gadgetry

Distance pedalled at a glance.

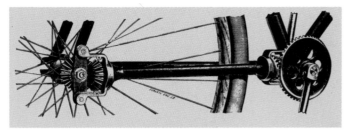

The chainless, gear-driven bike was heralded, then forgotten.

The kerosene lamp of elegance.

Do you Cycle
In the Summer?

You enjoy it, don't you? It saves doctors' bills and your temper; keeps your head clear and heart light, and helps you to enjoy life, don't it?

If your answer is

Yes

and you regret laying your wheel away for the winter, we want to invite your attention to the **McCready Ice Bicycle Attachment:**

A double-your-summer-fun kit.

SAFETY BICYCLE SUIT

PRICES OF SUITS, $5 to $15

"Safeties give with every move."

We want to draw special attention to our magnificent range of . . . .

Tandems

including :—

Bicycles built for two kept the woman in the driver's seat and the man heavy-pedalling.

hitching post.

In 1876, H.J. Lawson of Coventry, England, invented the sprocket wheel and chain for what was called the "safety" bicycle, and the front wheel was reduced to the same sane size as the rear. James Starley of England's Rover Company began commercial production of the safety bicycle in 1885, knocking dead a flourishing industry in tricycles which had sprung up to provide stabilizing wheels for people properly terrified to mount the high-wheeled "spiders."

thirst for novelty

John Moodie, the wealthy eighteen-year-old from Hamilton, Ontario, demonstrated the beginnings of a life-long thirst for novelty by importing and riding the first safety bicycle seen in Canada in 1878. Two years later Harry Goulding of Toronto imported five splendid "Silver Singers," and an awed *Canadian* magazine reported in 1881 that five daring wheelmen had cycled from Toronto to Whitby, Ontario, that spring, sensibly making the return journey by train.

There remained only the development of a pneumatic tire, the contribution in 1888 of John Dunlop, a Scottish veterinarian living in Ireland. A few years of weird and wonderful experimentation with frame design followed until it was clear that a trapezoidal frame was best. When ball bearings, hand brakes, adjustable handlebars and coaster brakes evolved, it was perfect.

The trapezoidal frame first appeared in 1890 in Paris, where some Frenchmen and even a few daring women were seen pedalling on the wooden drives and asphalt roads of the Bois de Boulogne. The bicycle at last was all things; thrilling, yet safe and comfortable. An entry in the annual bicycle race at Niagara Falls that summer featured the first pneumatic tires seen in Canada. Its owner, an Englishman, won his race by such a margin that when an American borrowed the bicycle for the next race, no one would compete against him. With that, bicycle madness gripped the country.

But bicycles imported into Canada in the eighties were expensive, costing more than a hundred dollars, a summer's pay for most working people. In the United States there were seventeen bicycle factories in 1890; by 1895 there were over three hundred. Some said bicycles had become the country's largest industry, yet Canada had no technology for steel tubing, bearings, rims or tires. The solution was assembly plants, importing parts from the United States and producing "Canadian-made" bicycles, bearing such lyrical names as the *Brantford Red Bird*. In 1895 Ottawa enacted tariff legislation aimed at stopping this practice. The result was the American bicycle companies moved across the border and set up plants in Canada.

The largest manufacturer was the Toledo, Ohio, company which made the *Cleveland*. It moved to a site west of Toronto called the Junction, stimulating the *Brantford Red Bird* plant to make its own bicycle parts. Massey-Harris in Toronto, makers of farm implements, promptly diversified and appeared in 1896 with the *Silver Ribbon* bicycle. A year later Canadian-made bicycles were being exported to the United States and England as well.

bikes for women, too

In September, 1899, Canada Cycle and Motor Company Limited was launched, a merger of Massey-Harris' bicycle division, the *Brantford Red Bird* people and three other firms. ccm blanketed the country coast to coast with high-quality bicycles that sold in Eaton's catalogue for as little as twenty-five dollars. For women cyclists there were dropped frames, the invention of an Englishman who wanted his bride beside him when he road-tested his vehicles.

Merrill Denison commented, "It was undoubtedly the bicycle that won for the nineties their present reputation for gaiety." The bicycle did more than cheer people up, it challenged the churches, revolutionized clothing and manners, and contributed to the emancipation of women.

better roads demanded

Bicycles were heady stuff. People wrote of them with such hyperbolic leaps of description as to see in them freedom, brotherhood and power. Postmen made their deliveries on bicycles, doctors pedalled to house calls. There were waiting lists at schools to teach bicycle riding. In winter, covered arenas were converted to bicycle tracks and tea was served while the band played.

Enthusiasts formed the Canadian Wheelman's Association, headed by Dr. J.W. Doolittle of Toronto. Doolittle and the irrepressible John Moodie vigorously lobbied for better roads for cyclists.

There was a bimonthly magazine, *Cycling*, devoted to the sport and cycling columns in every newspaper. In 1892 wheelmen from Toronto, Hamilton and other western Ontario centres pedalled to Chicago to take in the world's fair. The first Dunlop Trophy bicycle race at Woodbine race track in Toronto took place in 1891. The event drew a crowd of 12,000 to watch the twenty mile race, five around the track and the rest up and down Kingston Road. It became an annual event, abandoned only in 1926 when traffic congestion on Kingston Road made it impossible.

Every spring there were road races from one town to another. Groups of twenty to fifty rambled into the country for picnics or visits to country inns which hadn't seen such business since the stage coaches stopped running. Five hundred Sunday cyclists pedalled through High Park on a fine day. On the prairies cyclists looked from a distance like birds on a telegraph wire.

Riding with the times, Lever Bros. came up with a lucky monthly draw: 10 Stearns' $100-bicycles and 25 $25-gold watches – enough to keep kids washing behind their ears.

Proper young ladies didn't just get on a wheel and ride. Heavens, no! Beyond the basic problem of staying upright, there were rules of the road and etiquette that had to be learned. In the foul winter weather, Remington's was society's academy.

The *Whitby Chronicle* voiced a common complaint that out-of-town cyclists were boorish, taking over the best tables in local dining rooms and dominating the establishments with "bicycle horse-talk and loud body sweat and road perfume."

bicycle hooliganism

Bicycle hooliganism was in the news. On Saturday nights gangs of toughs pedalled into sleepy towns to create drunken havoc. But the country people had the last laugh – the absence of signposts on country roads put pedallers at the mercy of the natives, who amused themselves not infrequently by misdirecting whole platoons.

People went to work on bicycles, which allowed housing to extend beyond the streetcar lines and turned downtown areas into bedlam. Factories and office buildings were obliged to build bicycle sheds for employee vehicles, and stores had to make provision for cycling shoppers.

Bicycle accessories choked the market. There were cycling shoes, cyclometers, lamps for night cycling, repair kits for tires (an absolute necessity given the sharp-stoned roads), cycling suits for men (knickers and vented jackets), cycling goggles for use on dusty roads, and cycling camp kits.

Chaperones were the first conspicuous casualties of the bicycle craze. Since stout corsetted aunts did not take readily to the new contraptions, courtship and etiquette were revised. Women were free to test themselves against the exigencies of wind, weather and independence.

Their release from supervision was accompanied by a simultaneous release from binding clothing. Steel-ribbed waist-pinchers were intolerable for a cyclist and so were layers of petticoats and stiffeners. Bold women emerged in adaptations of Mrs. Bloomer's 1860 "Bifurcated nether garment" and caused the populace to swoon. There was such

outrage at the sight of bloomers that few women wore them twice. *Saturday Night*, sometimes a liberal journal for the times, was deeply offended for aesthetic reasons. "The female who wears them is a fright," it complained, adding that bloomers revealed "the most shapeless lot of legs ever seen outside a butcher shop." Canadian women settled for a modest compromise, a shortened riding skirt of thick cloth worn with knee-high gaiters.

The churches were shocked to discover Canadians preferred cycling to salvation. Since people worked a six-day week, Sunday was the only day available for out-of-town jaunts. Clergymen facing near-vacant pews in summer decried the bicycle as the devil's tool. Parents berated their children and employers glowered at their clerks, but nothing could intimidate a wheelman with a bicycle in the shed and his club blazer in the closet.

There was a brief attempt to impose rules of etiquette, so ritualized by Victorians, on the new cult. "The man doesn't mount until the woman is seated and ready to pedal," one set of instructions began. "Should strangers encountering one another on the road raise an arm in salute?" It was not required. "Should a man assist a woman stranger having trouble with her bike?" Yes, he might, and it was not improper for her to accept.

camaraderie of the road

It could not escape notice that bicycling was having a democratizing effect. The camaraderie of the road was resulting in touring parties mixing together along some stretches, rich and poor exchanging tips on bicycle maintenance and road conditions. Social barriers, when broken, had something to do with the craze for cycling.

The height of the bicycle rage was 1899. That year men took two-week vacations and pedalled up to six hundred miles. Cycling tourists, even with women in the party, clocked forty miles a day. Families went on cycling vacations and put up in hotels where bellboys parked the bicycles.

It was all wonderfully new and naughty but, as it turned out, doomed. There were already companies in both Canada and the United States turning out automobiles, the hottest new commodity on the continent. They were expensive, luxurious, comfortable – just what wealthy middle-aged men needed to give them the mobility of those pesky young cyclists.

Superstars and endorsements went together for the Goold Bicycle Company, sponsors of the fabulous Brantford Red Birds. The top "scorcher" of this star-studded team was Harley Davidson (no connection with the U.S. motorcycle company).

What does the well-heeled wheelman wear to complete his touring outfit? Why, ball-bearing bicycle shoes. Ball bearing bicycle shoes? It seemed like a good idea at the time for pedalling but an awful bother when walking up a hill.

Don't put your Daughter on the Stage

"Don't put your daughter on the stage!" had been the advice of busy-body relatives and friends for decades, but in the 1890s age-old wisdom and morality were on the run. Cities were growing, and with them the appetite of office workers and factory labourers for grand and tawdry spectacles of all kinds. The big-city stage was the dream of many naive young girls in those days, and some like these defied their grandparents, hoping some day to see their names in lights.

Julia Arthur of Hamilton was the rage of the stage, with her picture even on cigar boxes.

"An ideal Ophelia," Louise Beaudet was born in Montreal and educated at the Lachine Convent. Her mother took her to New York and put her on the stage.

Ethel Mollison of Saint John, N.B., made her debut in 1894 and rose to fame in road companies. Her first N.Y. hit was "The Cherry Pickers."

Daughter of an MP, Margaret Anglin was born in Ottawa's parliament buildings. She reached international stardom as one of the great emotional actresses.

Buxom May Irwin of Whitby, Ont., was the farce and burlesque queen of the nineties. At 25 she was earning $2,500 a week and made her million in comedy.

Margaret Mather grew up in poverty in Tilbury, Ont., and married Milwaukee millionaire Gustav Pabst. She played Juliet more often than any actress.

Caroline Miskell grew up in Toronto and went on the stage at 18. In 1897 she starred in "A Contented Woman," a hit melodrama typical of the era.

William Cruickshank's painting of his sister, Anne, is one of the finest character studies of 19th century Canadian art. The artist came to Canada from Scotland with his parents, but he received his training abroad, in Edinburgh, London and Paris. Returning to Toronto, he taught for 25 years at the Ontario School of Art. He was a strict instructor and often an outspoken critic of Canadian artistic values. He never married, and never made much money from work — "the eccentric old bachelor," he was called. It is only in recent years that his artistic genius has earned the recognition it deserves.

CHAPTER SEVEN

"Those New Women"

Why do women want to mix in the hurly-burly of politics? My mother was the best woman in the world and she . . . never wanted to vote.

Rodman P. Roblin, premier of Manitoba, 1900 - 1915

In the nineties a woman who complained that free land on the prairies was given only to men, or argued for the right to vote, was known as "one of those *new women.*"

When she spoke on a platform someone at the back of the hall was likely to shout, "Who's taking care of the children?"

In many cases, the nannies were; the "new women" tended to be those who could afford to be. Lady Aberdeen, for instance, had a title, was the wife of the governor general, and dined occasionally with Queen Victoria. Goldwin Smith described her as "the most aggressive busybody who ever presided over Rideau Hall," but her position gave her protection and authority enabling her to be one of the most effective feminists of the era.

In 1893, after the founding of the National Council of Women in Toronto, *The Empire* commented: "Hitherto it has not been the correct thing, from a Canadian society standpoint, for a woman to speak on a platform. But now for the first time a governor general's wife has given a public address."

Lady Aberdeen launched the National Council of Women that year, but she wasn't the only outstanding woman at that NCW founding meeting. On the platform was Adelaide Hunter Hoodless, the 36-year-old chatelaine of a four-acre estate in Hamilton.

Adelaide Hunter was a beautiful and brainy woman. Her father, a refugee from Ireland's potato famine, had died just before she was born on a farm near Brantford, Ontario. Her widowed mother raised twelve children, a struggle that taught several of them, including Adelaide, self-reliance and conviction.

When John Hoodless, son of a wealthy furniture manufacturer, proposed to her in 1881, she accepted. She was a strong Presbyterian and a Whig, marrying a man who was not only an Anglican but a Tory, but she stuck to her own religion and her own politics.

In 1887, John Harold Hoodless, her eighteen-month-old son, died. Mothers called the sudden fever that carried off infants and toddlers "summer complaint," and graveyards were dotted by miniature tombstones. Canadian families could expect to bury one child out of every five. But Adelaide wanted a better reason than "God's will." She found that farmers delivered milk to the city in open cans swarming with flies and heated by the sun, and her child, like hundreds of others, had died from contaminated milk.

Two years after her baby's death, at the first meeting of the Young Women's Christian Associa-

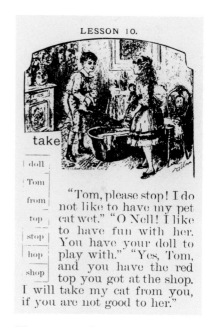

LESSON 10.

take

doll
Tom
from
top
stop
hop
shop

"Tom, please stop! I do not like to have my pet cat wet." "O Nell! I like to have fun with her. You have your doll to play with." "Yes, Tom, and you have the red top you got at the shop. I will take my cat from you, if you are not good to her."

The young Nells of the nineties let the Toms know that they wouldn't put up with pigtails in ink wells or cats in wash tubs, even in reading primers like this in the 1899 Empire series.

Curtain up! It's anyone's guess which fairy in this Peterborough pageant will reach stardom.

Rakish Mr. Parkes seems to be bending Miss Wolfenden's ear at this Victoria tennis party.

tion in Hamilton, the fledgling organization was unsure of its direction. Mrs. Hoodless suggested the cause of improved hygiene and nutrition. Under her direction as president, the YWCA developed cooking and domestic science classes for girls in school, and it was her influence in part that led to domestic science becoming part of school curricula and later a principal course of study in colleges and universities.

"eccentrics" at home

She was one of sixty Canadian women who journeyed to Chicago in 1893 for the Columbia Exposition, where women perhaps considered eccentric in their own communities, gathered to find like-minded women equally concerned with the vote, liquor legislation, education opportunities and working conditions for women. Lady Aberdeen was there, talking of national movements, and along with Adelaide Hoodless determined that groups, scattered loosely across Canada should unite. Mrs. Hoodless fired off some ninety letters upon her return to Hamilton and before year's end the first YWCA conference, representing twelve branches, met in Toronto.

That same year she wrote a guide book to nutrition, containing calorie charts and her strong recommendations in favour of fresh vegetables, meat and fruit in the diet. Known as "the little red book," it quickly became a kitchen utensil across the country.

Her finest achievement came about from a meeting on an evening in 1897. She was in an audience of farmers and their wives in Guelph, Ontario, listening to a lecture by a professor of bacteriology on the value of hygiene in the care and feeding of livestock. Adelaide was on her feet at once, raising her favorite question: what about the care and feeding of women and children?

Erland Lee, a farmer who headed a branch of

the Farmer's Institute, was impressed. He asked if women present would like to meet with him to discuss the founding of an institute of their own. The response was immediate, and on February 19, 1897, over a hundred women climbed the rickety stairs of Squire's Hall in Stoney Creek outside Hamilton. Adelaide Hoodless arrived in a carriage driven by her son, who sank down in a chair in the back row to be as inconspicuous as possible. Erland Lee presided and the first Women's Institute was formed that night.

Ground rules stipulated that Women's Institutes would stress homecrafts and motherhood: "Proper Food for Children" was the group's first pamphlet. Like the Farmer's Institute, Adelaide saw to it that it was federally funded.

Adelaide Hoodless died on her feet, giving a speech in Toronto's Massey Hall to the Federated Women's Institute. She was fifty-two years old. During most of her years, this "new woman" had contributed courage, determination and leadership to the struggle for equal opportunity for women. People in the audience that night said it was a vigorous, inspiring speech right up to the moment she collapsed.

WCTU fights for the vote

In Manitoba, where women needed little stirring up, the voice of protest tended to be the Woman's Christian Temperance Union. Originally a temperance group, by century's end they devoted themselves not only to the fight against booze but to the fight for the right to vote.

Prairie women were a tougher breed, perhaps more tested by loneliness and toil than women in the Eastern cities. Nellie McClung, raised on a farm near Brandon, once wrote of prairie women: "Many broke under the strain and died, and their places were filled without undue delay. Some man's sister or sister-in-law came from Ontario to take the dead woman's place. Country cemeteries bear grim witness to the high mortality rate in young women."

Conditions on the western frontier bound women together in mutual sympathy and made the Prairies the hotbed of women's opinion in Canada for decades to come. Women there saw widows disinherited from farms they had worked for years; saw free land given to men, even dissolutes and incompetents, but never to women; saw children abused or sent away by their fathers while the mother was powerless to intervene; and saw drink ruin men, devastate families and destroy farms and jobs.

a hilarious shocker

As the Woman's Christian Temperance Union saw it – as many western women saw it – the laws would never be changed until women could hold office and vote. Icelandic women, who in 1890 organized the first suffrage movement in Manitoba under Margret Benedictson, attracted prohibitionists from the beginning. In 1893 the WCTU staged a mock parliament in Winnipeg, composed entirely of women who debated male suffrage and used the same speeches parliamentarians employed against women's suffrage, with only the gender changed. The men in the audience were shocked, but it was hilarious all the same.

The "premier" on that occasion was Dr. Amelia Yeomans, the West's first woman doctor and a formidable campaigner for prohibition. She had seen the consequences in her years of exposure to the victims of alcoholism. That year, she had persuaded a member of the Manitoba legislature to introduce a bill granting women the franchise. When the time came for him to submit it, Amelia discovered that he had not even bothered to have it printed and had no intention of doing so.

Furious, she founded the Manitoba Equal Suf-

Adelaide Hoodless
The Farmer's Daughter

If anyone knew about the day-to-day problems and frustrations of farm women, Adelaide Hoodless did. She was born on a farm near Brantford, Ont., in the winter of 1857, one of twelve children. At the age of 24, she married a furniture maker and moved to Hamilton, but even as a city woman she maintained her close connection with the Farmers' Institutes. In 1897 at a meeting in Stoney Creek, she proposed the organization of a sister-group to the Farmers' Institutes, and a few days later formed the first Women's Institute. The idea spread rapidly, and by the early 1900s there were chapters across Canada. Mrs. Hoodless was also active in promoting education for women, and through her work many universities and colleges added degree courses in home economics to curricula.

"GRANDMA, shall I have a face like you when I get old?"
"Yes, my dear, if you're good."
— *Pick-me-up.*

. . . and did you hear the one about the husband telling his wife that he was making out his will: "Yes dear, and I'm giving you the full power to re-marry, because in that case I can be assured there will be at least one person who will daily mourn my passing."

Grip

Obviously the coach of the Edmonton Ladies' Hockey Club had no difficulty recruiting enough members to make up the team's "pom-pom" line and defense. The town's total population in 1899 when this photo was taken: about 2,000.

frage Society the following year, 1894, and bestowed on it the guileless motto *Peace on earth, good will towards men.* The group was an offshoot of the Dominion Women's Enfranchisement Association, formed in 1889, to which the redoubtable doctor also belonged.

Across the nation women were lifting their hemlines eight inches from the ground in the audacious American style, applying for admission to colleges, attending quilting bees in church basements, and returning home with some ideas that were quite different from those of their mothers. (Changes in women's fashion in many ways reflected the new freedom: the bustle was gone and the corset was soon to follow.)

There had always been job opportunities for single women from poor families. They could go to work as domestic servants or work in factories where they were appreciated because their fixed

wage was half that of a man's. Educated single women were finding employment as nurses or teachers. One woman in seven in Canada was working for wages, but almost invariably, women with paid jobs were single. Married women stayed at home. If they were in bad financial straits they took in boarders, laundry, sewing, or made hats.

The shock waves from the new women's movement were felt most acutely in what the newspapers called "well-connected families," where daughters were declaring that they wanted to attend a college or university. Arguments thrown against higher learning for women ranged from the benevolent solicitude that *women were too pure to be subjected to the coarseness of lectures on the human anatomy*, or a commonly held notion that *too much brain work drained energies from the reproductive system tending to create sterility.*

Women were being rejected by medical, engi-

In February 1892, when Edmonton was incorporated as a town, Matt McCauley was chosen its first mayor. This group portrait of his six daughters is a stunning fashion plate of young women's wear in the West in the nineties.

Carrie Derick
Miss Professor

neering and law schools across the country. Some of them determinedly travelled to the United States to be educated at colleges now admitting women. Others were turning to the new household science courses springing up in the wake of Mrs. Hoodless. Others such as Lillian Massey Treble, heiress to Hart Massey's fortune, founded schools of home economics at the University of Toronto and the University of Manitoba and contributed a great deal of her time to the success of women's organizations.

Many entered arts colleges. In 1897, only ten years after the first woman had been admitted in an uproar of controversy, one-third of the enrolment at University College in Toronto was female. That same year Queen's University in Kingston became the first in the country to offer a woman an honorary degree. The recipient, Lady Aberdeen, was amused to learn that there had been ag-

onized discussion as to the possibility of inventing some new degree, to be reserved for women, rather than granting her the customary LLD – doctor of laws. But when she appeared on the platform, male students in the balcony saluted her with a chorus of "For she's a jolly good fellow."

The traditional outlets of cultivated women, the arts, were replete with brusque, no-nonsense women. Naughty as it was, there were women on the stage. The Nickinson sisters appeared with their father in productions and Charlotte Nickinson later managed the Grand Opera House in Toronto. She was an emphatic founding member of the National Council of Women. Young Marie Dressler of Cobourg, Ontario, made her New York stage debut in 1892. Six years later Julia Arthur of Hamilton was touring the United States in Henry Irving's production of *Becket* with Ellen Terry, and hearing herself described as "the Sara Bern-

McGill University's principal was shocked! He had been dead against admitting women to the school from the first. But now, here was the top student in the class of 1888, Grace Ritchie, reading a plea for allowing women into medical school. If Carrie Derick wasn't at that commencement, she certainly heard about it. She was a sophomore at McGill that year, studying biology. A year after graduating she became McGill's first woman instructor, and in 1912 the first female professor in Canada. Born in 1862, throughout her life she was one of the most outspoken campaigners in the women's movement, and before she died in 1941, she saw women in virtually every legislature and university position in Canada.

EARLY SUMMER NUMBER.

VOL. XLVII.   No. 6.

THE Delineator,

A Journal

of

FASHION

Culture

and

Fine Arts.

DECORATIVE ART AS A PROFESSION, BY MRS. CHARLES SPRAGUE-SMITH, IN THIS NUMBER.

SOME HANDSOME BRIDAL COSTUMES ARE ILLUSTRATED AND DESCRIBED IN THIS NUMBER.

CANADIAN EDITION

Identical with that Issued by THE BUTTERICK PUBLISHING
Co. (Ltd.), 7 to 17 West 13th Street, New York.

Printed and Published in Toronto

BY

The Delineator Publishing Co. of Toronto
(LIMITED)

33 Richmond Street West, TORONTO, ONT.

JUNE.   PRICE. 15 CENTS.   1896.

As its graphic design suggests, The Delineator *was a "cultured" woman's mirror of the times.*

hardt of the American stage." May Irwin of Whitby, Ontario, who had made her debut at the age of fourteen, had reached stardom with her outrageous comic improvisations and was the most successful comedienne of her time.

Women novelists flourished. Joanna E. Wood of Queenston scored a brilliant critical success with *The Untempered Wind* in 1894, and Lily Dougall, educated at Edinburgh University and descended from Montreal's patrician Redpaths, imbued such novels as *Zeitgeist, Question of Faith* and *A Dozen Ways of Love* with social protest. But the hit of the nineties was Margaret Marshall Saunders' *Beautiful Joe: The Autobiography of a Dog,* published in 1893.

break into journalism

Formidable accomplishments indeed, but the arts had been open to women for centuries. In the nineties the real triumph was breaking into journalism. The Toronto *Globe* provided openings for some extraordinary women. Laura Bradshaw Durand wrote hard hitting editorials on international politics and war. As a sideline, she started the *Globe* book review department.

Sara Jeanette Duncan, Brantford-born, went from the *Globe* to the *Washington Post,* and then became the *Montreal Star's* parliamentary correspondent in Ottawa. Emily Cummings worked for the *Globe* for some years before becoming editor of "Woman's Sphere" for *Canadian Magazine.*

Another *Globe* writer, Ella Elliott, moved to the *Toronto Evening News* after marrying that paper's editor, Joseph E. Atkinson, in 1892. In Montreal, Robertine Barry, using the by-line "Francoise," was the witty editorial writer on *La Patrie.* Catherine Simpson-Hayes from Regina moved to the Winnipeg *Free Press* to edit a page for and about women, which she declared "filled a crying need."

The list was growing by the year. There was

Cora Hind, who was becoming world renowned for her ability to predict the yield per acre of the entire western breadbasket with such accuracy that the world wheat market paid attention. W.A. McLeod of the *Western Producer* once said of her, "Miss E. Cora Hind was rather terrifying. She was more positive about everything than most people are about anything."

flair for the sensational

Another woman journalist people paid attention to was Kathleen Blake Coleman, who headed a department called "Women's Kingdom" in the *Toronto Mail and Empire*. "Kit" – as she was known – was the world's first woman war correspondent, wangling her way with guile and gumption into the front lines of the Spanish-American war in Cuba. A scandalized army officer sent her packing and she found herself on a ship jammed with mutilated, dying soldiers. She worked with surgeons operating on the exposed deck and wrote about that too. Irish-born, with a flair for the sensational, she covered the Chicago and San Francisco Fairs and Queen Victoria's Diamond Jubilee in London, and launched an editorial campaign against corsets that worried Toronto merchants.

The changing attitudes of women in the nineties had effects on more private matters as well. Family life, which had retained the status of a sacrament, imbued with religion, was dedicated to duty, sacrifice and loyalty. On the subject of sex, *Lancet*, the most respected of British medical journals, published a learned paper explaining that women by nature did not enjoy sex, unless they were prostitutes. Clergymen and school teachers attacked sex for purposes other than having children as not only sinful but dangerous to health and sanity, likely to result in depraved offspring.

Courtship was under severe control in order to confine sexual expression to sighs and meaningful

Most well-to-do single women like Miss Arnton did not work; there was no need. Until marriage they lived at home, dabbled in cultural activities, and took part in club socials and sports.

Sara Jeanette Duncan
Cousin Cinderella

It was unheard of – two young ladies traipsing around the world with no chaperone! and Miss Duncan knew it. She called her book *A Social Departure,* and when it reached the bookstores readers were delighted. Sara Jeanette Duncan was born in 1862 in Brantford, Ont., taught school for a short time and then decided to invade the man's world of journalism. In 1891 she married a museum curator from Calcutta and left to live in India, but never forgot her girlhood. She wrote a dozen more books, the best of which, *The Imperialist* (1904), is a witty and brilliant portrayal of life in a "squat and uninteresting" town in turn-of-the-century Ontario. Before she turned her writing to foreign subjects, she treated her Canadian readers to one more book: *Cousin Cinderella: A Canadian Girl in London* (1908) – a bon-bon that mirrors her own Cinderella life.

looks. At puberty, and literally overnight, a properly-raised girl stopped wearing children's dresses and her hair loose on her shoulders. She lowered her skirt hem, pinned up her hair, and became her mother's satellite. She could go nowhere alone. Even engaged couples could not appear at a ball or theatre without a chaperone, usually a dignified and preferably married aunt. When a couple sat in the parlour, a younger sister or brother was assigned to stay in the room. What wickedness there was followed bribing the child to leave for a few minutes.

The proprieties enforced upstairs exploded downstairs. Lady Aberdeen muttered in her journal about the mistreatment of women servants; the seduction of young women was the theme of Victorian pornography. Illegitimate children were rendered almost invisible by the deep disgrace and family rejection suffered by the unfortunate women. Weekly journals in Canada had standing ads for "comfortable homes for ladies before, during and after accouchement. Infants adopted if desired. Strictly confidential."

Babies of unmarried mothers usually were placed in "baby farms." Some nursing mothers there fed babies other than their own, but there were always too many babies for the number of wet-nurses. Since infant formula and bottle-feeding were unknown, many babies placed in baby farms died of starvation, disease and neglect.

Extreme forms of birth control were unusual, but there was an underground exchange of contraceptive techniques among women. Even some bootleg copies of a famous book, *Physical, Sexual and National Religion* were available. Written by a

forthright Scot, Dr. George Drysdale, the volume had chapters on most methods of birth control known today.

An 1893 marriage manual, *Courtship and Marriage*, by Rev. A.S. Swan, cheerily assumed that procreation was under control. He was all in favour of limiting family size. "Every woman wanted a son, and a home was incomplete without a daughter, but what need was there for more?"

The problem was far from solved, however. Adventurous as some women were in the era, few could pursue careers after their marriages unless they were infertile or their husbands wealthy enough to afford nannies. But single women were gaining college entrance and jobs with increasing regularity. A subscriber to *Canadian Magazine* wrote in 1893 to complain that some two hundred women had taken jobs in Ottawa. He saw no other reason for it than "cupidity, selfishness and pride," and fumed that soon there would be nothing left for husbands and brothers but housework.

A debate raged for three months in the letters to the editor column of *Saturday Night* when a woman, signing her real name, wrote that marriage should be suspended for twenty years to permit society to re-evaluate its merits. Letters signed "Happily Married" poured into the columns, followed by a wave from an entrenched down-with-marriage contingent revealing a depth of resentment and simmering in Victorian kitchens.

People began to predict that the social structure of the family could not tolerate the new woman. The institution would collapse, and bring society down with it. No good, they said, could come from such a change.

The Notorious Mrs. Chadwick

Cassie Chadwick was the last of many names Betsy Bigley signed in her life. The others, all involving some forgery, hoax or con game, eventually put her in prison, but until her death in 1907, she lived a cunning and extraordinary life. She was born in 1859 in Eastwood, Ont., the daughter of a railway worker. At 13 she was arrested for passing cheques on a fictitious family fortune. At 16, as *Emily Heathcliff,* she managed a brothel in London. As *Lydia DeVere,* she worked as a clairvoyant in Cleveland, and in 1882 cast her spell over Wallace Springsteen, a doctor. Betsy cleaned him out in no time, and he filed for a divorce. In 1890, as *Florida Blythe, heiress,* she was arrested for forgery and spent three years behind bars. She was madame in a Cleveland bordello when Dr. Leroy Chadwick walked in and swept her away to Euclid Ave., the city's millionaires' row. Betsy quickly frittered away the Chadwick fortune, then concocted the story that she was Andrew Carnegie's illegitimate daughter. Exhibit A at her sensational six-day trial was a cheque for $250,000 bearing the signature of Carnegie (a good forgery); exhibit B was the multi-millionaire himself. It was her last grand stand before jail.

She charmed a dozen men out of their fortunes.

Her cell was outfitted in Victorian finery.

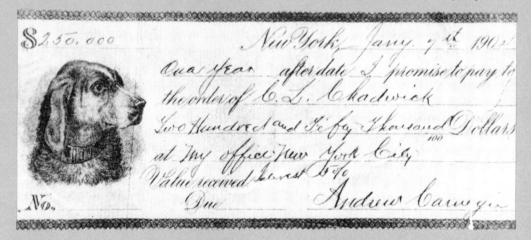

Found among her papers was a second cheque with Carnegie's signature for $5 million.

SEARCH ✦ON✦
LIGHTS HEALTH

Light on Dark Corners.

A COMPLETE SEXUAL SCIENCE

—AND—

A GUIDE TO PURITY AND PHYSICAL MANHOOD.

Advice to Maiden, Wife, and Mother.

LOVE, COURTSHIP AND MARRIAGE.

BY

PROF. B. G. JEFFERIS, M.D., PH.D.,

AND

J. L. NICHOLS, A.M.

TWENTIETH EDITION

J. L. NICHOLS & CO.

PUBLISHERS AND IMPORTERS

TORONTO, - CANADA

Light on Dark Corners

Sex? Respectable folk didn't discuss it, and curious youngsters had to stumble their way to knowledge – unless, of course, they first stumbled across this "guide" in a corner of father's study. Like many others of its kind, *Light on Dark Corners* was an imported, plain-brown-wrapper kind of best-seller, but modern readers will find only dim light here. Victorian morals abound in its pages: old wives' tales, Biblical sermonettes and straight-laced views. Could our grandparents really have been so unenlightened? Judge for yourself: "Man is a careless being, very much inclined to sinful things . . . To be more than an animal, man must be able to resist all instinctive impulse by exercise of self-control . . . Strive for mental excellence, and you will never be found in the sinks of pollution and the benches of retailers and gamblers . . . Beauty is shallow, dangerous, deceitful, reigning only to ruin, gross – leading often to sensual pleasure . . . Woman is by nature more chaste in thought and language . . . No sensible young man with a future will marry a flirt . . . Any improper liberties will change love to sensuality and affections will become obnoxious if not repellent . . . Never marry a man that does not make his mother a Christmas present . . . Marry in your own position in life . . . Red whiskered men should marry brunettes . . ."

Beginning Right,

The Beginning of Life.

1. **The Beginning.**—There is a charm in opening man-hood which has commended itself to the imagination in every age. The undefined hopes and promises of the future —the dawning strength of intellect—the vigorous flow of pas-sion—the very exchange of home ties and protected joys for free and manly pleasures, give to this period an interest and excitement unfelt, perhaps, at any other.

THE RESULT OF BAD COMPANY.

ASKING AN HONEST QUESTION.

6. **Ladies' Society.**—He who seeks ladies' society should seek an education and should have a pure heart and a pure mind. Read good, pure and wholesome literature and study human nature, and you will always be a favorite in the society circle.

90

HOW MANY YOUNG GIRLS ARE RUINED

Flirting and its Dangers.

1. **No Excuse.** In this country there is no excuse for the young man who seeks the society of the loose and the dissolute. There is at all times and everywhere open to him a society of persons of the opposite sex of his own age and of pure thoughts and lives, whose conversation will refine him and drive from his bosom ignoble and impure thoughts.

2. **The Dangers.**—The young man who may take pleasure in the fact that he is the hero of half a dozen or more

History of Marriage.

1. "It is not good for man to be alone," was the Divine judgment, and so God created for him an helpmate ; therefore sex is as Divine as the soul.

Giving a Parlor Recitation.

Disadvantages of Celibacy.

Keeping Bachelor's Hall.

The old Bachelor sewing on his Buttons.

THE TWO PATHS.

WHAT WILL THE   BOY BECOME?

IDLENESS AND IMPURITY.

INDUSTRY AND PURITY.

VICE AND DISSIPATION.

HONORABLE SUCCESS.

MENTAL AND PHYSICAL WRECK.

HONORABLE OLD AGE.

Letter Writing.

Any extravagant flattery should be avoided, both as tending to disgust those to whom it is addressed, as well as to degrade the writers, and to create suspicion as to their sincerity. The sentiments should spring from the tenderness of the heart, and, when faithfully and delicately expressed, will never be read without exciting sympathy or emotion in all hearts not absolutely deadened by insensibility.

DECLARATION OF AFFECTION.

Dear Nellie: Will you allow me, in a few plain and simple words, respectfully to express the sincere esteem and affection I entertain for you, and to ask whether I may venture to hope that these sentiments are returned? I love you truly and earnestly, and knowing you admire frankness and candor in all things, I cannot think that you will take offense at this letter. Perhaps it is self-flattery to suppose I have any place in your regard. Should this be so, the error will carry with it its own punishment, for my happy dream will be over. I will try to think otherwise, however, and shall await your answer with hope. Trusting soon to hear from you, I remain, dear Nellie, Sincerely Yours,

J. L. Master

To Miss Nellie Reynolds,

In large part, it was advertising that sold the Canadian West to the world, and among privately-owned companies, no promotional campaigns were more enticing than those of Massey-Harris. In this good-humoured calendar cover, Canada may be cutting the cake but Miss Massey-Harris is passing out the pieces. Being in the business of manufacturing ploughs and harvesters meant that a good year for the farmer was a good year for the company, and the more farmers there were, the more implements could be sold. With sales agents across Europe, doubtless this picture of Canadian prosperity abroad added a few farmers to the growing list of immigrants.

CHAPTER EIGHT

The West to the Rescue

If a settler is one who has been engaged in agricultural pursuits . . . it is most desirable to encourage him to occupy our land. . . .

James Smart, deputy minister of the interior, 1900

There was gold in British Columbia and in the Klondike, fields of golden grain on the prairies where immigrants were beginning to cut furrows in the buffalo grass. Although Toronto and Montreal controlled the economy and the railways, the mood of enterprise and confidence that swept Canada at the end of the 19th century blew out of the West.

The Métis and Indian threat to western expansion had been snuffed with Riel at Regina and the prairies were open for settlement. Edmonton could now joke about the weeks it waited for battle, tribes massing on the outskirts, cut off from communication with the rest of Canada after Riel cut the only telegraph line.

The Indians were back on reserve lands, kept there by Mounties and clergymen they trusted. Schools were established and farm implements distributed, a function requiring the office of an Indian agent appointed by Ottawa. For the most part the agents were romantic, cultivated men who immersed themselves in native culture. The Comte de Cazes, an Indian agent overseeing five reserves in the Edmonton region, commented glowingly on the honesty and energy of Indians and their facil-

ity for acquiring industrial skills. Around Fort Qu'Appelle, native people had prosperous farms and their children were learning carpentry and harness making. In 1891 the NWMP reported that the Blackfoot, Sarcee and Stony around Calgary seemed settled and happy: horse-stealing and cattle-killing had become rare. Parents were proud of their children's accomplishments in school which included a student brass band at High River. The Blood and Peigan, it was said, were able farmers. The Sioux left behind when Sitting Bull was forced back to the United States, were working amiably at odd jobs around Moose Jaw.

At the urging of Mounties and clergy, the plains tribes had given up most of their traditions. The buffalo hunt was just a memory, and with it had vanished a style of life, religion and ritual that dated back hundreds of years.

The Ghost Dance was another matter. The dance lasted four or five days and was performed by both men and women, some in white Ghost shirts decorated with feathers, bones, arrows, birds, suns and stars symbolizing that time when the whole Indian race, living and dead, would be reunited upon a regenerated earth.

In 1890 the demoralized tribes on the plains and along the west coast were swept by a conviction that the Ghost Dance that summer would roll the white races off the continent and restore the land to the natives. They danced with a frenzy that

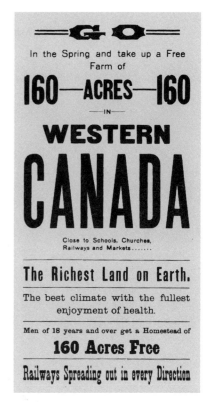

The offer was accepted by thousands in Russia, Europe and the States. They found the soil dry, growing time short, and winters long. Not all of them succeeded, but many carved a life, then a living from the land.

The old way of life has passed. An Indian father in clothes that have seen many summers sends his children in prim and pressed uniforms to the Qu'Appelle, Saskatchewan Industrial School.

gave a clear message of their frustration, and brought down reprisals in both Canada and the United States. The dance was condemned and outlawed, Ghost Dancers were arrested. As suddenly as it had flared up, the Ghost Dance was extinguished.

tribal morale shattered

The winter of 1892 marked a turning point for what appeared to be a promising transition. That year Commissioner Herchmer of the N W M P wrote to Ottawa, "We have had very little trouble with the Indians . . . the most willing workers we have." But the winter was bitterly cold, followed by a crop failure in the summer. With money short in the West, tempers and prejudice flared. Native farmers were trapped – they could neither make a living nor move. Alcoholism hit the reserves. The following year, with Canada slipping into a depression and another bad crop in the West, the morale of the near starving, destitute tribes was shattered.

The original Indian agents were replaced and the new men were often small-minded despots who flaunted their authority. There were reports of atrocities. One agent refused medicine for a sick child, who died. The grieving father, a Blackfoot, shot the agent and was shot himself by a Mountie. Some clergymen, established on the reserves as missionaries, developed traits akin to feudal lords. A Catholic priest, Father Chirouse, was jailed for having a Lillooet woman whipped for her sins.

By 1897 the country had recovered from the economic doldrums but it was too late for the western tribes. Mounties wrote that the natives were saying that they "may as well die by the white man's bullet as of starvation." Indians were drinking heavily and stealing from neighbouring farms. Herchmer wrote, "The lazy, loafing life they are compelled to lead, even the exercise and excitement of the chase having been swept away, is the greatest incentive to crime and outrage."

Rev. John McDougall, who spoke Ojibwa before he spoke English, was a brawny man who had come to the West from Ontario as a youth. He could run all day in light deerskins behind a dog-sled at forty below. A friend of the Blackfoot and other tribes, McDougall came forward with a warning, "They are in despair. They find themselves robbed of their manhood. They are placed far below the plane conceded to the basest and vilest and most degenerate of white people."

Lady Aberdeen, crossing the prairies on a vice-regal tour in the late nineties, wrote:

Miserable specimens in dirty, squalid, coloured blankets haunt the railway stations, with the object of selling buffalo horns or baskets of feather work. . . . It is a pathetic sight to see what appears to be ghosts of a people of other days, stealing gaunt and mournful and silent to the towns and railway stations. . . .

They are an unattractive sight, with their deeply-lined countenances and prominent feathers, bedaubed often with paint, their black dishevelled hair, their array of ragged, squalid blankets or tattered garments to which fragments of tawdry finery give the finishing touch to an aspect of distasteful wretchedness.

settlers by the thousand

By the end of the nineties the railways were spilling settlers on the big flat land by the thousands. They became part of the complexities and contradictions of the West. The mix of decency and exploitation, compassion and viciousness stood out in sharp relief against the aching clarity of the huge sky.

It was a land of contrasts and the weather pro-

Like his fellow plainsmen, Peter Wesley faced an uncertain future in the white man's world. His forefathers were horsemen, hunters and warriors; he would seek work wearing a coat, shirt and tie.

95

Ernest Brown's Wild West

Just after the turn-of-the-century, a young photographer arrived in Edmonton with five dollars and a ticket home in his pocket. He had apprenticed in England, developed an interest in the West, and worked his way from Toronto to see what all the excitement was about first-hand. His first job was with C. W. Mathers, a superb but footloose cameraman, and within two years Ernest Brown had bought Mathers' entire file of glass plate negatives. To this and other collections he added his own work: the finest record that exists of the people who passed through and settled the West.

Ernest Brown peers proudly from behind a vast array of cameras, equipment and lenses. These large, temperamental devices recorded the history of the West.

Gun and knife toting American Klondikers posed in Mathers' studio.

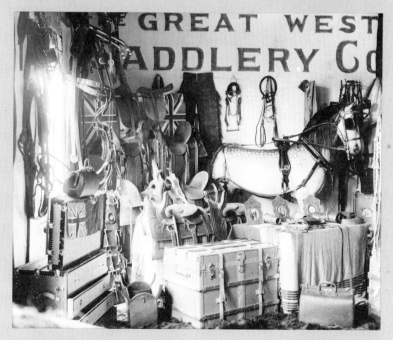

A Sarcee poses in every bit of fur and feathered finery found in the studio.

A promo shot for Great Western Saddlery — the genteel wild west.

**Sam Steele
The Law in the Yukon**

In the powder-keg gold-rush days of Dawson, Sam Steele ruled the town with an iron hand. He was a big man, limber as a cat, and his presence was enough to ease the sleep of bankers and honest miners. He wouldn't tolerate profanity or cheating or disorderly conduct, and even censored the occasional bawdy stage show. He was born in 1849 in Purbrook, C.W. (Ont.), the son of a military man. At age 15 he served in the militia during the Fenian raids, in 1870 went west with the Red River Expedition, and was one of the first officers in the RNWMP. In 1885 he became superintendent of the force. From the Yukon he went to Africa, and in the Great War led the 2nd Canadian Contingent as major-general. When he left Dawson, instead of the blue one-way ticket he had dispensed to trouble-makers, townsfolk gave him a poke of gold.

vided the most heartless one of all. "During the long, cold winter, it seemed that all our effort and energy were spent in just keeping alive," wrote Sarah Ellen Roberts in her journal *Of Us and Oxen*, "but when the spring came life seemed to take on deeper meaning, and we felt we were a part, even if a small one, of a greater purpose of awakening, of creation and of growth."

Some people were enlarged by the hardship and achieved heights of generosity. The stark land was acquiring a reputation for open-handed hospitality but few showed concern for the spectres of buffalo hunters crouched in rags at railway stations. It was as though they weren't there.

"mushroom" towns born

It didn't escape notice that the taming of the Canadian West proceeded in a style totally different from the opening of the American west. The countries' western frontiers, exploding side by side in places, provided dramatic illustration of the contrasts between a country born of revolution and one born of counter-revolution; between a country dedicated to the freedom of the individual, a melting pot of patriotism, and a country that was an uneasy mosaic held together with authority. On one side of the border were men who made their own laws with guns. On the other side were "mushroom" towns, built around churches and police posts.

Rossland, a mining camp in British Columbia, was such a town: home to two thousand miners, almost all of them from the United States. It had but one policeman, John Kirkup, and didn't require more. Kirkup confiscated every gun in town, icily staring down all protests from men for whom guns were as natural as hands. He had no jail, nor felt the need of one.

He was not unique. A single NWMP constable routinely met the cattle drives that swept through

the middle of the continent and ended in Alberta. He would greet cowboys from Texas and Montana civilly and ask that they put their gun belts in their saddle bags and keep them there until they re-crossed the border. First-time herdsmen were amused, then skeptical, but there was something about the Mountie's calm conviction that was more persuasive than force.

In the United States there were still Indian wars. In 1890 the 7th Cavalry surrounded some starving Sioux at Wounded Knee in a surprise raid and killed three hundred. In Canada the Mounties controlled native unrest without firing a shot. They were not unaccustomed to riding into a tipi encampment alone. An entry in the NWMP annals describes a small band of Mounties who found themselves surrounded by angry Bloods. Though one Mountie was wounded and dying, their orders were to refrain from shooting. They kept their guns in their holsters and stared impassively at their tormentors until the Bloods withdrew.

Hilliard gets his man

Another incident concerned Staff Sergeant Chris Hilliard who in 1891 rode after two Blood Indians, The Dog and Big Rib, who had escaped from jail. Hilliard arrived at the Blood village just as a Sun Dance was in progress. He was surrounded by furious braves who threatened to kill him if he touched The Dog, but Hilliard, without hesitation, seized him. He said to the Blood chief, "There will be no backing down." The men measured each other a long moment. Two hours later The Dog was back in jail in Fort MacLeod.

The Klondike gold rush again demonstrated the difference between Americans and Canadians in their raw state. In the summer of 1897, when the world rang with news that there was gold in a northern river called Klondike, the stampede of explorers, poets, drifters, crooks, strivers and fools

Klondike Gents and Ladies

Big Moose Alex McDonald became "King of the Klondike";
Frank Cushy peddled ten thousand bottles of bug repellant;
Arizona Charlie Meadows ran a portable bar on the trail;
the Rag Time Kid tickled the ivories at the Dominion Saloon;
Nellie Lamore bit off a bartender's ear for insulting her;
and Diamond-Tooth Gertie packed her nugget belt with gold.

Hard-luck miners like Charlie Ainsworth at the 60-Above claim played solitaire while Silent Sam Bonnifield and the Oregon Jew staked thousands at poker.

The Trail of '98

Up the rivers and over the peaks they came –
prospectors, prize-fighters, Yankee buncos,
English aristocrats, newsmen, prostitutes.
Dozens of trails led to fortune or famine:
steamer from Seattle up the Yukon; dogsled
over glaciers; horse and mule team over the
White and Chilkoot Passes; flatboat up from
Edmonton; overland across bogs and tundra.

Dressed for the occasion, two "gold-diggers" joined the pick-and-shovel crew at a Klondike sluice.

One of the girls with a heart of gold.

There were enough American fortune hunters in Dawson in 1899 to warrant a flag-flying Fourth-of-July celebration, with all roof-top and pole seats taken.

The Klondike News *proclaimed the bounty of '98 with George Carmack, discoverer of Yukon gold, flanked by two nuggets: the largest is over two pounds.*

was on. Within a month of word reaching Seattle, nine thousand people left for the Yukon by boat.

The reality of the North came as a shock. A few wanderers and some fur traders had seen it, but for the most part, the forbidding land had been left to the hunting tribes who had lived close to the Arctic for centuries. Here the cold was so piercing and abrupt that even a rushing river would freeze. Mountain passes were mantled in glittering ice and little food could be found on the land. Confusion, panic and despair accompanied the gold rush.

carried their weapons

Skagway, on the Alaska panhandle, was the port of entry for those who came by sea. Their destination over White Pass and Chilkoot trails was Dawson City, deep in the Yukon Territory. These two towns were as different as night and day. Skagway was one of the wildest, most disreputable communities; Dawson a bastion of law and order.

Almost on the day the rush began, there was a mass execution in Skagway with one corpse left to dangle in public view. After that grim beginning, men carried their weapons day and night. People became adjusted to the sound of gunfire and to bullet holes in their tents. Superintendent Sam Steele of the Mounties—a man not given to exaggeration—called Skagway "little better than a hell on earth."

In Dawson on the other hand, guns were forbidden. There were no murders. Non-payment of wages, dog-stealing or using vile language constituted a crime. A man could leave his cabin door unlocked for weeks and return to find nothing touched, not even a poke of gold.

Steele was a genuine folk hero—unflappable, brave, intelligent, incorruptible and tough. On his orders, prospectors who didn't bring a year's supply of food with them were turned back at the

Canadian border, a ruling which saved lives and prevented exploitation of the hungry.

Prospectors in a hurry to reach the gold fields after the spring thaw of 1898 attempted to run the rapids, a recklessness which took ten lives and destroyed 150 boats before Steele arrived on the scene. Edgy, glowering men had created a bottleneck of rafts and boats, some of dubious buoyancy. A mood of violence hung over the tangle. Steele faced the stormy crowd with commanding assurance. No boat would be allowed through without an inspection for soundness, he said. Women and children would not be endangered; they would walk on the banks of the river until the craft was safely through the rapids. It was sane and sensible, and that's the way it was done.

The other tranquilizing force on the western frontier was religion. Rev. Robert McCahon Dickey arrived in Skagway early in October, 1897, an Irishman newly graduated from Manitoba College and burning with a zeal to be of use to others. He had persuaded the Presbyterian Home Missions to send him to the Klondike to spread the gospel, but was so anxious to get started that he had to be ordained en route to Vancouver.

built his own church

He found Skagway appalling. It was then a tent city of some five thousand, almost all male. He had never seen a gun fight. With serene resolve, he set about building a church. His first fund-raising attempt was a benefit concert, which included performing dogs and a trio known as the Montana Flats. Aided by occasional volunteers, he built the church with his own hands, cutting the trees for it himself, and in December it was open for services.

He called it Union Church. The Skagway newspaper in the spring of 1898 contained a church notice: "There will be services of all kinds and at all hours in Union Church tomorrow. Take a day off and go to church." Sundays started with a Roman Catholic service at nine, a Protestant service along simplified lines after that, and an Episcopal service next. In the evening Dickey conducted something he called "the Union service."

He was big, friendly and did not pass judgment – attributes which reduced much of the friction a Skagway clergyman might otherwise have faced. When he married a miner and a dance-hall girl, he made a mild comment in his diary: "May God help them to keep their vows." Without comment he buried men who had been shot to death and babies whose deaths did not appear natural. He had little concern for his own safety, once trying to calm a lynch mob, another time rescuing an Indian who was being beaten by thugs.

hard on miners

In the spring of 1898 he walked over the long graveyard known as White Pass and pitched his tent on Bennett Lake. There was plenty for a clergyman to do. Funerals kept him busy at first – so many miners died from exposure or typhoid. He made weary mention in his diary of the victims of a Chilkoot avalanche and later a poignant note about a miner found dead with his face turned to the photograph of his wife. "Hard place on ministers," he wrote tersely.

He then moved on to the gold fields. There was no time for church building now. On Sundays he conducted services in the streets of Dawson, standing on a beer barrel with "the girls" lounging on the brothel balconies above him. During the winter he made regular rounds of the miners' cabins, though temperatures often dipped to forty-six below and his health was failing.

Dickey received orders to leave in 1899. The gold rush was already subsiding. As he passed through Skagway, he found Union Church still

Robert Henderson
Hard-Luck Klondiker

The quest for gold had consumed 23 years of Robert Henderson's life. He was the son of a Nova Scotia lighthouse keeper, and had panned and picked for gold in Australia, New Zealand and Colorado before wandering the Klondike's creek beds. In 1896 he staked his claim at Gold Bottom Creek just south of Dawson and missed the greatest bonanza of them all by a few miles. That year he met "Lying George" Carmack, an American misfit who was friendly with local Indians. Henderson and Carmack agreed to exchange any news of strikes they heard, but a few days later when Carmack struck it rich at Rabbit Creek, Henderson was left in the cold. Prospectors flooded into the area, but Henderson's claim was too late. Beaten, bitter and suffering bad health, he sold his claims for a paltry $3,000 and boarded a steamer for Seattle.

Clifford Sifton
Promoter of the Last Best West

Free Homes for Millions! The Last Best West! 160 Acres Free Land in Western Canada! . . . It was a razzle-dazzle campaign, and behind it was a born promoter. Clifford Sifton was appointed minister of the interior in 1896, the first westerner to fill a cabinet post. He was 35, a lawyer from Brandon, Man., and a no-nonsense business-man. His first action was to re-vamp his department and spell out its policies: he wanted steady, honest, sober and willing-to-work farmers, rich or poor, English, French, Russian, American, what-ever. No city-folk need apply. The campaign was one of posters and painted wagons and newspaper ads – 6,000 rural U.S. papers carried them. Some foreign governments were irate and banned the agents and their leaflets. Nevertheless, the flow of immigrants increased: from 17,000 in 1896 to 141,000 in 1905, when Sifton resigned the post.

standing but the multi-denominational congrega-tion torn by feuds. On the ship to Vancouver he overheard passengers mocking his seedy, worn clothes. He said nothing but consoled himself in his diary, "They can't understand a man doing work for any other motive than personal gain."

The Reverend lived a good, mellow life, a preacher in the region of Hamilton, Ontario, until his death in his seventies. His sweep of the country from Manitoba to the Klondike had taken him through the heart of economic vitality that was re-storing hope across Canada. There was a sense of release and energy everywhere. Suddenly immi-grants weren't talking of moving on to the States as soon as they got their wind, and Canadians were deciding to stay too. Nothing much had changed, and yet everything had changed.

Clifford Sifton, a lawyer from Brandon, Mani-toba, took over the Department of the Interior in 1896, determined to turn the West into the nation's breadbasket. By the end of the century his campaign to recruit farmers was working. There were 100,000 sod-busters on the plains, Dutch, Ice-landers, Finns, Norwegians, Germans and Russ-ians. The Maritime provinces and Ontario were sending families. The West meant opportunity.

Most of them stuck with that dream, though the absence of building materials meant that they started in huts made of cut sod, sleeping under umbrellas and oilcloth when it rained. They rocked their babies in cradles made of jute sacking and the women planted geraniums in tin cans on the windowsill.

Getting there was half the agony. Maritimers

who travelled the trail to Swan River, northwest of Dauphin, Manitoba, in 1898, describe a road that was 110 miles of mudholes. For a generation after, western winters were livened by freighters arguing the relative demerits of that Swan River road and the one to Peace River, both memorable horrors. Swan River veterans maintained that no gumbo could be stickier or deeper, joking that it once swallowed a horse whole.

They moved at the rate of ten miles a day, and the trail was littered with furniture, binders, mow-ers, rakes and cartons abandoned to lighten the load. At the end of the road was Hugh Harley, running the land office in the midst of all the tents and selling bread for 75¢ a loaf on the side.

It was a little easier on people who came in the winter, travelling by sleigh along the land cleared for that prairie necessity, the railroad. By that time, Hugh Harley was living in a log house with open porches on three sides, Victorian gingerbread running amok. The town project in Swan River on Arbor Day in 1899 was to pull the tree stumps out of the main street.

Canada's project was to finish the job of haul-ing itself out of the hard times and it was doing it handily, perked up by golden promises from the Klondike and the Prairies. Wheat exports bounded from two million bushels in 1890 to al-most seventeen million in 1900. There was so much bustle in the West that people wanted more railways. Wilfrid Laurier was on the point of yield-ing. "We cannot wait," he said, "because at this moment there is a transformation going on which would be folly to ignore and a crime to overlook."

Long leather belts and exploding steam boilers were a hazard to life and limb, but the Shackleton brothers and their Alberta farmhands are enjoying the rig.

CHAPTER NINE

The Licence to Practise

One of the first duties of a physician is to educate the masses not to take medicine.

William Osler, M.D.

Dr. William Osler had departed McGill's medical faculty in 1884 for more honour and reward at the University of Philadelphia, but despite the loss to Canada of one of the outstanding medical minds of the nineteenth century, Montreal was still in its golden age of medical exploration. Medical training had been lengthened to four years, and students were having their brains rattled with a deluge of medical breakthroughs.

Microscopic examination of blood and tissues had partially unravelled the mystery of disease. Diptheria inoculation was available, though most people were frightened to have it. In Quebec there had been riots against efforts to make inoculation compulsory. In the wake of Lister and Pasteur, major surgery could be attempted without risking death from post-operative infection. Cocaine was being used as an anaesthetic in Vienna for nose and throat surgery, enabling pioneer work on sinusitis. A London surgeon, Victor Horsley, operated on brains and spines with some success, though few could believe it. Another doctor in Germany developed a method of cutting through chest walls and removing obstructing ribs to aid in clearing lungs clogged with emphysema.

Joseph Lister's Canadian disciples had introduced his principles of sterile, safe surgery to Canada more than a decade earlier to considerable resistance. The method depended upon a carbolic spray machine which drenched the wound and surrounding area throughout the operation (and sometimes enthusiastic operators drenched doctors, nurses and visitors as well). German surgeons had taken to wearing rubber wading boots while operating and visitors kept their feet dry by standing on chairs.

Surgeons grumbled at the messiness of the technique but the carbolic disinfectant truly opened the age of surgery, cutting down mortality rates dramatically. Further refinements of sterile procedure were on the way. In 1896 a surgeon in Breslau designed a face mask to wear while operating. A Berlin doctor a few years earlier established a routine of boiling surgical instruments before operations and wore a sterilized cotton gown over his street clothing during surgery. Johns Hopkins' brilliant William S. Halsted noted the complaints of his favourite nurse, who protested that pre-op scrubbing of her hands in mercuric chloride was giving her a skin rash. In 1889 he went to New York and consulted with the Goodyear Company, which produced the first rubber surgical glove. The grateful woman married him.

The other major barrier to the success of surgery had been pain. By the nineties, ether and

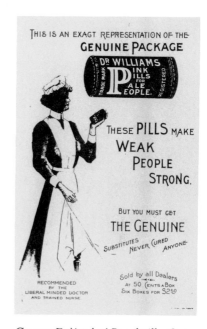

George Fulford of Brockville, Ont., made a fortune with these "pink pills for pale people." A staunch Liberal, Laurier appointed him to the Senate. (Note the message above, bottom-left.)

Opposite page: *Some of these med students at Queen's University look a little pale themselves at mid-autopsy. (Pass the pink pills.)*

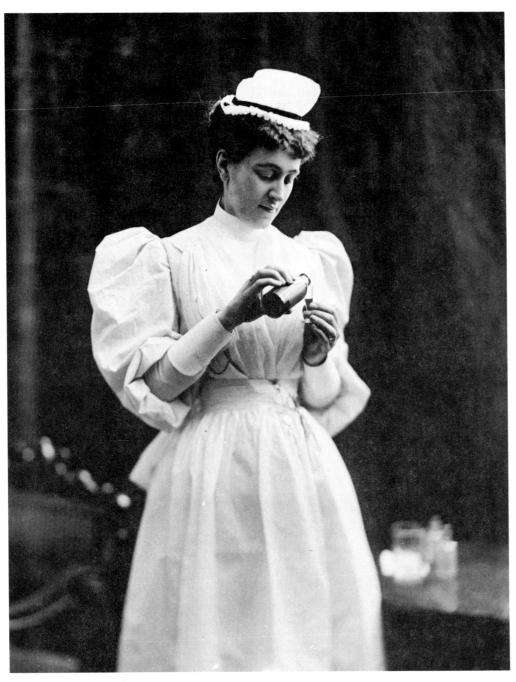

Nurse Pettigrew's uniform is spotless and right in vogue with period styles. By the nineties nurses' training and hospital conditions had improved, but the 12-hour shift was a standard.

chloroform were in general use, enabling such complicated procedures as bowel resection.

In 1895 Wilhelm Konrad Roentgen, a professor of physics at Wurzburg in Germany, announced "a new era in physics." He had discovered the existence of high-frequency "x-rays". All substances, he noted, are more or less transparent to x-rays. On February 7, 1896, only weeks after receiving the news, Montreal's doctors were using x-rays to scan broken bones. Montreal, the first city in Canada to equip a laboratory with microscopes, is believed to have been the first in North America to use radiology.

the new specialists

The excitement of the scientific frontier attracted to medicine some of the brightest and best minds. Doctors who responded to the cracks and fissures opened by the new technologies soon found themselves specialists. In the nineties, little St. Joseph's Hospital in London, Ontario, listed on its staff surgeons, gynecologists, obstetricians, ophthalmologists, pediatricians, pathologists, homeopaths and anaesthetists. When McGill University's Faculty of Medicine offered a summer course in 1897 for doctors to update their skills, it included such subjects as heart disease, otology, dermatology, genito-urinary surgery, orthopedics, laryngology and mental disease.

The Canadian Medical Association, which had considered disbanding because provincial medical societies left it little function, had an enrolment leap between 1893 and 1899 of 363 doctors.

The explosion in medical science was creating a need for more hospitals in Canada. For three centuries hospitals had been used only by those who were either desperately ill or poor. The high mortality rate had given the community the impression that hospitals were places designed for dying. People avoided them in horror and instead were treated at home by doctors and nursed by their families.

Doctors making their rounds from house to house travelled light. The tools of the trade, outside of simple medicines, were a stethoscope, a clinical thermometer, bandages, forceps, amputation saws, lancets, surgical needles and thread. Surgery was confined to the removal of abscesses or the amputation of gangrenous limbs; operations were performed on kitchen tables or in the hospital operating theatre. A few doctors had operating rooms adjoining their offices, but this meant sending post-op patients on an agonizingly jolting carriage ride home.

The development of sterile, painless surgery necessitated expensive equipment, and since patients were now likely to survive, beds and nurses had to be nearby. It meant a new life for hospitals, and a new outlook on hospitalization. Some communities wanted hospitals so badly that almost any convenient building would do. Moncton General Hospital opened in 1898 in what had been a poor house. Calgary General Hospital began in 1895 in a building someone had punctured with bullet holes, and when Brandon General Hospital opened, it was dependent on a windmill for its water supply.

nurses' training

The profession of nursing bloomed along with the growth of surgery and hospitals. Doctors had been in the habit of asking anyone handy to keep an eye on their patients. Cooks and scrub women learned how to change bandages and apply fever-cooling cloths, but sophisticated medicine required more. A four-month training period was instituted, which soon grew in bounds until nurses were taking three-year training courses and studying anatomy, emergency surgical procedures and post-op techniques. They learned to apply intricate band-

ages and, since there was no adhesive tape, prodigious amounts of gauze and cloth were used. Nurses worked twelve-hour shifts. At night, they looked after patients alone.

Hospitals entered cheerily into the Victorian fondness for uniforms and each had a distinctive costume for its nurses. In the Montreal General they wore pink, and the Toronto General staff turned out in brown and white gingham.

Osler brings changes

Medical training for doctors was undergoing a profound change too, not only in the length and variety of the subjects covered but also in the introduction of clinical experience. William Osler had become the continent's chief spokesman against the established method of teaching entirely in lecture halls. Students graduated without ever attending a real patient or seeing a baby born. Osler complained that graduates "would not know a Scarpa's space from a foot," and added, "Is it to be wondered that quacks, charlatans and imposters possess the land?"

Undergraduates began visiting hospitals, watching surgery and prodding live abdomens, but still much of their knowledge of anatomy depended upon dissecting cadavers. Ancient taboos against the violation of the dead were converted into law. In Canada only executed criminals were legal subjects for pathology. Historically surgical advances tended to coincide with wars, which provided ample subjects, but in peacetime medical students resorted to robbing graveyards.

In 1890 the *Montreal Gazette* protested "A Ghastly Sensation at Kingston; Grave-Robbing Medicos," and described how the keeper of a cemetery had surprised Queen's University students as they were opening a coffin. One student was shot, but the rest escaped bearing several bodies with them. The police later discovered one of the miss-

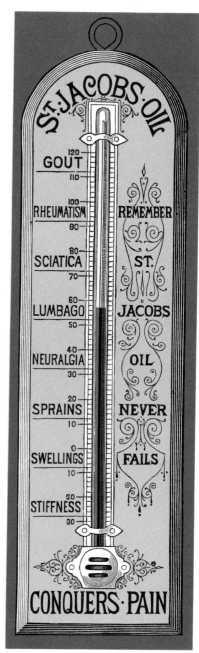

St. Jacobs and hundreds of similar oils made the "intemperate" claim of curing all manner of diseases, everything from stiffness to gout.

PAINE'S Celery Compound

For The Nervous
The Debilitated
The Aged

Wells, Richardson & Co.
Montreal.

Celery compounds, it was claimed, could cure any headache in town.

The names were enough to send shivers up and down your spine! Datura Tatula Asthma Cure, Keating's Worm Bonbons, Edison's Obesity Salt, Kilmer's Swamp Root . . . few of them tried to sugar the pills, elixers, compounds and quack medicines on the shelf.

THE GOOD DOCTOR

Milburn's Heart and Nerve Pills – just what the doctor ordered!

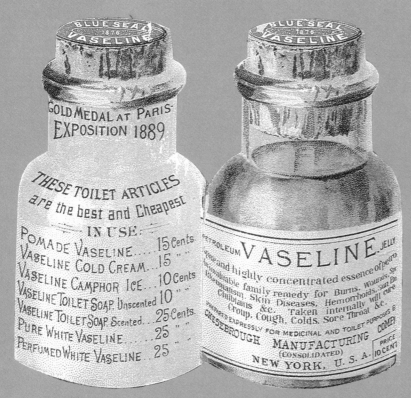

As the label says, Vaseline taken internally cured coughs, sore throat. . . .

Before science took over the field, many nostrums were bastardized Indian remedies.

AYER'S SARSAPARILLA

The DEACON: "Land sake Liza, the very sight of that bottle makes me feel like another man."

AYER'S SARSAPARILLA IS A COMPOUND CONCENTRATED EXTRACT-THE STRONGEST, BEST, CHEAPEST BLOOD MEDICINE.

Sarsaparilla was among the most vaunted tonics of the cure-all era.

The first Japanese families settled on the B.C. coast in 1878. By 1901, 4,738 had entered the province. At Steveston's Japanese Hospital, Drs.Robinson and Oishi tended to these fishermen.

ing cadavers in a college building. "A horrible sight," they commented.

McGill students stealing bodies in winter from a graveyard on Mount Royal would lash them to toboggans. One student would sit on top of the grisly load and ride it to the bottom. Aspiring medical men had the presence of mind to undress the corpses at the grave-side; stealing a clothed cadaver would involve extra charges of theft of personal property.

operated on lunatics

Meanwhile surgeons were experimenting with living subjects behind the walls of asylums for lunatics. A substantial number of physicians believed that insanity was caused by organ disfunction. In women the guilty organ was often believed to be the uterus, hence the practice of hysterectomies. Others thought the seat of madness was the brain, and accordingly attempted neural surgery. Some believed that castration would help.

One of the great reformers of psychiatry of the nineties was Dr. Richard Maurice Bucke. During an adventurous youth Bucke lost a foot and part of the other to frostbite. Though never formally educated, he entered medical school and graduated from McGill in 1862. He joined the profession at a time when insanity was regarded as something not human. Mentally ill people were known as "aliens," beings beyond feelings or hope kept in barred cells until they died.

Like his predecessor, Dr. Joseph Workman, a pioneer in psychiatry in Canada, Bucke discarded chains, stopped the practice of drugging mental patients with alcohol, and established work programs in the asylums.

He founded a medical school in London, Ontario, was its first professor of Nervous and Mental Diseases, making the distinction between neuroses and psychosis, and went on to become president of

112

the American Medico-Psychological Association, later of the American Psychiatric Association.

Despite such sources of enlightenment, the practice of medicine in the nineties was generally far from scientific. Most doctors relied on hunches and experience, which taken together were not much improvement over the wisdom of grandmothers and home remedies. People tended to doctor themselves with patent medicines whose common effective ingredients were morphine or alcohol. Diseases with mediaeval names still wiped out entire families.

In 1891, a year when the entire population of Canada was little more than four million, 7,000 Canadians died of tuberculosis, almost 4,000 of diphtheria and 1,500 of typhoid. European immigrants that year brought a cholera epidemic to the East; in the West an outbreak of smallpox was traced to a Chinese laundryman. In New Brunswick, a new lazaretto, a hospital for the poor, was built to relieve the wretched condition of the leper colony at Tracadie. The disease had been striking down Acadians since 1836.

from morphine to heroin

For the most part, doctors fumbled in darkness. Routine treatment for patients complaining of abdominal pain was a strong purge, bringing disastrous consequences when the pain was caused by an inflamed appendix. Morphine was prescribed for pain, and laudanum, a tincture of opium, was the basis of "soothing syrups" given to babies. Arsenic and belladonna were recommended for nervousness and strychnine for alcoholism. Opium addiction was a recognized problem, the solution to which was to wean the addict by administering morphine. A generation later, morphine addicts would be treated with heroin.

Indian herbal remedies were much admired, as were traditional home medicines such as bread

"Home Remedies"

ASTHMA
A muskrat skin worn over the lungs with the fur side next to the body.

BLEEDING AND CUTS
To stop blood, bind on goose feathers and press them into the wound. Allow them to remain until they come off.

DROPSY
Lobsters dried in an oven and reduced into powder are a great use against dropsy, if that powder is taken by a patient every morning – in some white wine.

EPILEPSY
Take some wheat flour that will mix with dew, gathered on the morning of St. John's Day; make of it a cake, which being baked, give it to the patient, and he shall be well.

ST. ANTHONY'S FIRE
Bathe the affected parts with laudanum or lead water, or dust them with rye meal or wheat flour.

GOUT
The severest fits of gout will, it is said, be cured by the suffering if a maggot is worn enclosed in a flannel cloth near the skin.

JAUNDICE
Take some goose dung and soak it in some white wine during twenty-four hours, then strain the whole, put a little sugar in it, and the patient must take this potion.

LOCKJAW
Fill a pipe with tobacco and cover the bowl with a rag and blow the smoke through the stem into the affected part.

NASAL CATARRH
For nasal catarrh or hay fever, take the black soot out of a wood stove, tie in a thin cloth and pour boiling water over it. Gargle and draw through the nose.

CHILBLAINS
Bear grease, mixed with a little alum, cure likewise the chilblains in the heels as well as the cracks in the hands.

COLDS
Mix one-fourth ounce of gum camphor in one-half teacup of goose oil, put on a flannel around the throat, and also rub it on the nose.

CORNS
Rattlesnake or mud turtle oil will, applied a few nights at bedtime, eradicate corns.

DEAFNESS
Drop rattlesnake oil in the ear once or twice a week.

MALARIA
Sulphur placed in the shoes during the summer season will be absorbed into the system and keep mosquitoes or fleas off and will thereby prevent malaria.

SORE THROAT
Slice a piece of old smoked bacon, the older the better. Stitch this to a piece of old flannel and make it black with pepper. Warm it and fasten it closely around the throat.

TOOTHACHE
Burn a piece of paper on an old plate, then with a small wad of cotton, wipe up the brown sweat on the plate and plug it into the tooth.

"Doctor" H. G. Root probably gave himself the medical title. Men with little or no medical training still passed themselves off as doctors, often treated patients in strange and dangerous ways, and gave their names to worthless pills and cures.

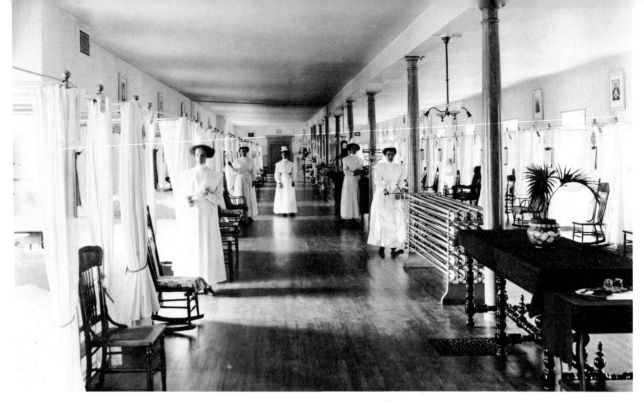

Nurses make their rounds at Montreal's Hôtel Dieu. In the '90s nursing was thought the ideal profession for women.

poultices and mustard plasters. It was said that water was safer to drink if a few rusty nails were added. Some people sewed themselves into underwear in the fall and took it off in the spring. Standards of cleanliness were not high in any case, as many people thought baths were weakening.

The struggle against infectious diseases seemed hopeless. The microscope had opened the way for understanding their contagious nature but there was little co-ordination or leadership to implement that knowledge. The Canadian Medical Association lobbied the government to establish controls to prevent the spread of such communicable diseases as tuberculosis, but it was a common sight on crowded streetcars to see someone cough blood into a stained handkerchief. When diphtheria struck one child in a poor family, it was certain to spread to others, since the sick child would continue to share a bed with two or more sisters and brothers.

A medical journal in 1897 proclaimed the discovery, *Consumption Now a Communicable Disease*, but it wasn't until the end of the decade that Canadian cities passed regulations requiring that cattle be inoculated against tuberculosis as a first step to safeguarding milk. Pasteurization had not yet been introduced.

Doctors were far from ready to co-operate across provincial lines. Boundaries were so rigid that a doctor in Hull, Quebec, would be fined by his medical society for consulting a doctor across the river in Ottawa.

Few cities had begun to clean up the open cesspits in slums. When Quebec City abolished them in 1893 and updated the sewage system by replacing wooden drains with tiles, the death rate that year was cut in half. Most communities dumped raw sewage into whatever lake or river was convenient. In summer even well water became polluted and typhoid epidemics raced through many

114

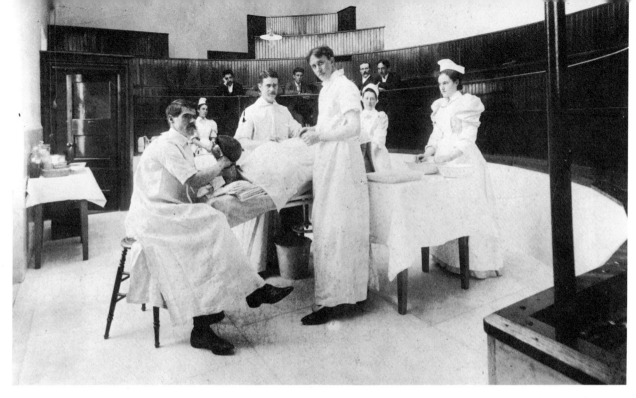

Nobody's wearing masks, caps or rubber gloves during this operation at Montreal's progressive General Hospital.

Dr. Koenig makes modest claims for his drops. Some maintained their elixir would cure anything from cholera to "vitiated blood," a common complaint of the day.

communities.

Robert Kirk, in the Yukon during the gold rush, wrote: "Dawson never found time to build a sewage system and the filth that accumulates during the long winters and then lies exposed to the decomposing effect of the warm sun in summer is, in great measure, the cause of the prevalence of malarial-typhoid fevers that are epidemic in June, July, August and even September and October." He noted that "several hundred" died of fevers in the summer of 1898. Tappan Adney, also in Dawson that summer, commented: "By midsummer the hospital was filled to overflowing, men were lying on the floor, and there were many in cabins suffering from typhoid fever, typhoid-malaria and dysentery. The number of deaths was three to four a day, in one day reaching a total of nine."

People who railed against such conditions were no longer seen as cranks. There was a growing awareness that disease could be prevented. When

four children in one family in Barrie, Ontario, died of diphtheria, their father sued the town for $100,000, charging their deaths were due to civic neglect.

Provinces established boards of health in response to complaints. Staffed by sanitation inspectors and a doctor on a part-time basis, they were overwhelmed by the enormity of the problem and their own lack of authority. The federal government was being pressured to enter the health field, a provincial jurisdiction. There was a growing feeling that a federal department of health was needed to deal with the nationwide epidemics.

Lady Aberdeen, addressed the problems with a plan to relieve some of the nation's health problems by campaigning for the establishment of a Canadian Victorian Order of Nurses to make home visits. A similar organization existed in England to deliver health services economically to the poor. It seemed to her equally necessary in Cana-

**Amelia Yeomans
The Doctor's Wife**

She was a doctor herself, and the wife of a doctor, but the only work she wrote was publically burned in Winnipeg: *Warning Words,* an honest and straightforward tract on sex. Controversy was nothing new for Amelia Yeomans. After her husband died in 1878, she applied for admission to medical school but was turned down. She went to the U.S., graduated, and in 1885 set up her practice in Winnipeg – the West's first woman doctor. She was 43. When a group of Icelandic women first organized for women's rights in the Prairies in 1890, she saw it as a breakthrough, and in 1894 she founded the Manitoba Equal Franchise Club. Its cryptic motto: "Peace on earth, good will toward men." She was a prominent leader of the WCTU and women's groups until she died in Calgary in 1913.

da, particularly in the West where isolated Prairie families rarely, if ever, saw a doctor.

The National Council of Women supported her proposal with a petition and Lady Aberdeen forged ahead. Outraged doctors saw visiting nurses as a menace to their incomes, and the Ontario Medical Association termed the Order "a broadside on the land." The Winnipeg Medical Association said it would prove "an entire failure." The *Canadian Journal of Medicine and Surgery* predicted that the country would be depopulated of doctors and professional nurses who would leave to work in the United States.

The superintendent of the Toronto General Hospital, Dr. Charles O'Reilly, roused support among Conservatives to defeat the Liberal plan to grant the Victorian Order of Nurses a federal charter. He argued with such conviction that the country already had too many medical practitioners that Laurier withdrew his support.

Lady Aberdeen summoned reinforcements. A Harvard graduate in medicine, Albert Worcester, had founded a school to train district nurses. She invited him to Ottawa to meet twenty-five doctors at a reception. (She observed that they were pleased and astonished to be served liquor instead of tea). Worcester was persuasive in Ottawa and even more effective when he met 200 doctors in Toronto.

By the time the VON received its charter, May 19, 1898, four intrepid nurses had already left for the Klondike, walking the more than two hundred miles from Telegraph Creek to Dawson. They had signed three-year hitches at a $350 annual wage.

The VON was not the only significant health service born in the nineties. Following years of

shaky existence as a project started in 1875 by Elizabeth McMaster and a women's committee, Toronto's Hospital for Sick Children moved to new quarters.

In 1896 the Canadian Red Cross Society came into existence, and in 1900 the Canadian Association for the Prevention of Tuberculosis was founded. Ontario established the first provincial health laboratory in Toronto to prepare diphtheria antitoxin. At about the same time, Alexander Graham Bell was founding the first Canadian chapter of the Home and School Association, which was to play a role in improving the health of children.

In 1892 Wilfred Grenfell, an Oxford-trained doctor, twenty-seven years old and determined to spend his life wherever he was most needed, arrived in Labrador in the ketch, the *Albert*, loaded with medical supplies. Fishermen on that bleak coast were without medical services. Among his first patients was a case of beri-beri, a vitamin deficiency disease few doctors ever encountered. Labrador suited his purpose exactly. In the first two months after his arrival, he was swamped with nine hundred patients needing urgent attention.

That winter Grenfell was running behind a dogsled to bring medical help to isolated Inuit. In the years that followed, his dedication not only established the Grenfell Mission, an up-to-date hospital, but also brought schools, children's homes, and other welfare services to a part of the country previously deprived and practically ignored.

"This is an age of advances and progresses," a prominent Canadian doctor, W. Grant Stewart, told graduates of Bishop's College near Sherbrooke, Quebec, in 1893, "and no science is making greater strides than medicine."

A patient's patience was sorely tried in the days before motorized ambulances. This rig is setting out from Victoria General in Halifax, N.S.

CHAPTER TEN

Lady Aberdeen's Diary

As soon as she arrived it was like the Palace of the Sleeping Beauty. Everything that had been dead and dusty came alive. . . .

Catharine Tynan on Lady Aberdeen

A country is its people, and in the nineties the citizens of Canada were an odd lot.

There were those outside the corridors of influence: the poor, the disobedient, French-Canadians, women, most Catholics and Jews, Indians. And there were those who thought of themselves as the backbone of the nation: solid British stock on the good farmland, businessmen with stylish shaven faces, shopkeepers of devout and thrifty habits. These latter gave the country its tone of innocent pomposity, delight in simple, family pleasures, and a sweet sense of righteousness.

But weaving in and out were all sorts of wonderful individuals salted with a sense of their own worth: prophets, scoffers, upstarts, reformers, rogues and charmers who were the bane and blessing of their time. Some were suave and some prickly; some rode all their lives on the leading edge of change; some were scoundrels and some were brave. What they had in common was that they were uncommon people, vivid and out-of-step; and they wrote their country's history.

Foremost among them was Ishbel Maria Marjoribanks, who was thirty-six when she arrived in Canada in 1893 as Lady Aberdeen, wife of the new

governor general. A British aristocrat capable of chilling hauteur when she chose, she was also generous, impulsive, observant and empathetic. She launched the Irish cottage weavers, for instance, and insured their success by taking their wares to the Chicago World's Fair where they were sold for $100,000 profit. She headed the Scottish Mothers' Union, the Women's Local Government Society, and the International Council of Women, all of them hotly controversial feminist organizations. She established correspondence courses for women servants and lectured women workers on their rights. On Friday nights she stood on street corners in London and invited prostitutes to have tea with her in the Strand Rescue Mission.

At twenty she married a "Fighting Gordon," the sixth Earl of Aberdeen. He was a charming, quirky man, so fond of trains that he was said to be the only peer in the realm who could drive the train from Edinburgh to London. (He was also an avid collector of recordings of train whistles.)

The Aberdeens arrived in Canada with four small children and ambitious plans to tour Canada from coast to coast. They did that—travelling part of the way in a canoe—and more. They were untiring in their willingness to accommodate Canadians. In Prince Albert, the Earl of Aberdeen gave ten speeches in a single day; his wife proudly noted in her diary that each was different. He presided at the opening of a creamery in Renfrew,

The modern woman of the nineties found Massey's Magazine *a monthly forum of new ideas and opinions.*

Opposite page: *The great engineer, Casimir Gzowski, and his wife pay a visit to the governor general's. Lord Aberdeen (front left) and his wife, Ishbel (centre) introduced a "shocking" informality to the viceregal post that is not apparent in this rather stiff, formal photo.*

All aboard! Well, almost everyone. When Ottawa's street-railways were electrified in 1891, the gents hopped on the open car and dusted off their bowlers. Any familiar faces in the crowd?

Ontario, and drove in a carriage through the terror of a wild prairie thunderstorm to visit an isolated Indian agent by night.

They bought a ranch in British Columbia and a summer home in Quebec. And the intrepid Aberdeens did not hesitate to ride bobsleds or logs down a timber chute. They had the aristocrat's conviction of unshakable dignity which freed them to try anything.

unstuffy meddler

All their travels and observations went into Lady Aberdeen's journal, faithfully kept for five years even on those days when she gave birth. Historians have called it the most important single manuscript of the period. In it Lady Aberdeen reveals herself to be a cheerful, stubborn, sentimental, unstuffy meddler, liberal in her views and impetuous in her behaviour.

She was an observant and blunt reporter. She noted that servant girls in the West were well paid ($20 a month, the highest wages for "domestics" in the country); that weavers in Quebec's Eastern Townships used onion skins to dye woollens yellow and goldenrod to deepen the shade; and the cost of catering a reception in Toronto, which was twenty-five cents a head, covered ices, strawberries and cream, the waiters, silver and crockery, but *not* claret and sauterne.

She said in Regina, "No one lives here who is not obliged." When Presbyterians sent missionaries into Quebec to convert Catholics, she commented: "If they would make the Protestants *Christians* and as moral as the Roman Catholics, they would advance their causes quicker." And she described a Boston woman as "one of those rare beings in the United States – a lady."

She had equally pronounced views about leading Canadians. She liked William Van Horne, a next-door neighbour when the Aberdeens took up residence in Montreal; she noted that Lady Thompson cooked parliamentary dinners herself to save money while her husband was prime minister; she noted that the wife of Manitoba's lieutenant-governor, J.C. Schultz, was a liar.

She put in her journal everything that interested her, and she was both curious and observant. She described cariboo herds in the North, so numerous that it took days for them to pass. She described Chinese cooks on CPR ships who dressed in white and wore pigtails down their backs. She saw Saskatchewan in the spring–"the mud and its adhesive qualities is something to be remembered."

Canadian women wore blue veils on sunny days to "avoid being freckled." The mayor of Ottawa, a former lumberman, went to city hall in a blanket coat and wearing snowshoes. Mark Twain, on a platform in Victoria, had the strangest, sloppiest sort of head at the back, with long hair about his neck. She noted that it didn't snow in Ottawa until January during the winter of 1896-97, and that the following summer her daughter Marjorie counted 107 mosquito bites on her person.

rescued the outcast

According to her journal, the Aberdeens loved two Canadian prime ministers, Thompson and Laurier, and detested two others, Bowell and Tupper. She rescued the "notorious" Mrs. Foster, wife of the minister of finance, who was a social outcast in Ottawa because she had been divorced; Lady Aberdeen invited her to Government House and ended a freeze imposed on the hapless woman by John A. Macdonald's puritanical spouse.

From the time she arrived in the country in 1893, Lady Aberdeen was determined to launch Canadian branches of two international women's organizations: the International Council of Women and the Victorian Order of Nurses. Ferocious opposition from such adversaries as the religious and medical establishment would have nipped both organizations in the bud, if Lady Aberdeen had not quieted the fears of Victorian Canadians.

In 1893 she summoned to the initial planning meeting of the National Council of Women professional women from various clubs and their husbands, plus a selection of women she had met and liked. When they convened and met one another they were aghast. Her excellency had committed the ultimate social error by inviting not only Catholics and Protestants to the affair, but also Jews, Quakers and Unitarians.

difficult to digest

The ladies also learned that the International Council of Women, which had branches in the U.S., England and Scotland, was non-denominational. It was formed in the belief that women should work together across individual differences, of whatever kind, in order to improve their common lot. The grandeur of the concept was difficult for Canadians to digest so rapidly. Lady Aberdeen only narrowly staved off a constitutional amendment to exclude "the godless," by which the women meant all non-Christians.

Opposition then came from Quebec bishops who didn't want Roman Catholic women associating with Protestants. But Lady Aberdeen found in Toronto's Archbishop Walsh a liberal who didn't mind his parishoners joining the ICW and one who was willing to say so. Next she negotiated with the tremulous Catholic women who were reluctant to join because they were certain Protestants would snub them. Finally the NCW was ready for its founding meeting. It almost floundered on the opening prayer.

All meetings in Canada began with "God Save the Queen" and an opening prayer. It was unthinkable to deviate from the ritual, but what

**Henri Julien
The By-Town Minstrel**

Laurier sang, coat tails flapping (see p. 56); Sifton danced a jig; Cartwright dozed at his desk; and other parliamentary notables made up the chorus in Henri Julien's caricature Ottawa ministrel show, the "By-Town Coons." For each new session, Julien would leave his wife and sixteen children, set up studio at the Russell Hotel, and work into the early morning hours translating the day's events into the week's cartoons. Born in Quebec in 1854, he had mastered the art of on-the-spot drawing working for the Legg Bros. and *Canadian Illustrated News*. At 20 he went west with the Mounties on their first trek to Fort Macleod. Back in Montreal, he joined the *Star* in 1888 as a political cartoonist and art director, and devoted his free time to sketching and painting.

The Lighter Side

THE DIVERSION OF THE SEX.

Mr. Quigly—"Where'r you off to, Jennie?"
Mrs. Q.—"I'm going shopping."
Mr. Q.—"What are you going to buy?"
Mrs. Q.—"Buy? Why, nothing, of course. I'm only going shopping, you stupid fellow."

HIS DIFFICULTY.

Hostess—"Oh, Mr. Podge, are you not going to dance?"
Mr. Podge—"Certainly, my dear madame, I shall be very happy—if you can find me a concave partner."—*Sydney Bulletin.*

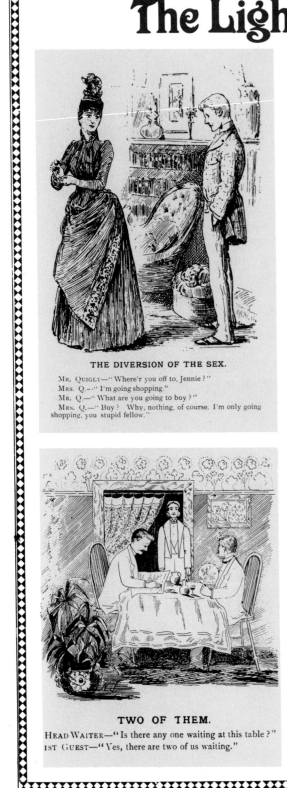

TWO OF THEM.

Head Waiter—"Is there any one waiting at this table?"
1st Guest—"Yes, there are two of us waiting."

PUZZLED.

"Now, blamed if I can remember whether I was to meet Agnes on Elizabeth street or Elizabeth on Agnes street."

---

prayer would embrace the faiths of every woman in the room? It appeared hopeless until someone had the inspired suggestion that a *silent* prayer be offered.

A newspaper headline the next day proclaimed: NATIONAL COUNCIL OF WOMEN AGAINST LORD's PRAYER. Lady Aberdeen commented, with restraint, that the banner was not particularly helpful.

quit over a prayer

The next meeting of the NCW was equally stormy. A good many members wanted the silent prayer to be followed by the Protestant version of the Lord's Prayer recited aloud. The vote on this divisive issue was close, 56 to 45 in favour of silent prayer alone. Women representing the Protestant Orphan's Home in Toronto promptly resigned, followed by other indignant Protestants.

Despite the intensity of that mean-minded wrangle, the National Council of Women became a reality – not subversive of women's responsibilities in society, but mindful of a greater role women were capable of playing in public life. As Lady Aberdeen told the Montreal audience:

There is one thing of which I should like to remind you, and that is that in attempting this work we are most anxious to have it remembered that we do not desire to overlook the fact that woman's first duty and mission is to her home. People sometimes speak as if. . . woman's first mission in itself prevented her from taking part in public work. They forget that a woman, if she is to do her duty. . . must keep touch with the world, its thoughts, its activities, its temptations.

Lady Aberdeen was as tough physically as she was in spirit. One chilly spring afternoon her carriage slipped off the road into the ice-strewn Ottawa River. The horses were swept away and drowned and the weight of her heavy skirts was pulling her under as her rescue was effected. She then walked briskly home in her wet clothes, changed and promptly wrote letters of assurance to relatives and friends. She presided at a dinner party for Laurier that evening and was later received at a formal ball for senators and MPS.

Her most remarkable triumph occurred just before the Aberdeens departed Canada. They had promised Britain's Prime Minister Gladstone that they would live a short time in each of Canada's major cities, but even their high principles around duties had not been enough to compel them to include Toronto in that group. They disliked the city which had been cold to them and much preferred Quebec, Montreal and Halifax.

But time was running out, and they concluded that they would have to take up token residence in Toronto. Lady Kirkpatrick, wife of Ontario's lieutenant-governor, was not fond of the Aberdeens and united Jarvis Street society against them. It was difficult for them to rent suitable accommodation. The city was rife with stories that they were too casual with their servants, that the Earl of Aberdeen played cards with the cook. Toronto Tories bore a grudge because they had opposed Tupper, and Toronto Orangemen could not forgive that they were friendly to Catholics. Temperance advocates were affronted that they served liquor.

Lady Aberdeen observed: "The only thing to do was to go straight ahead as if totally unconscious of the opposing forces." They blandly met with Goldwin Smith, who had publicly called them puppets and had urged Canadians to abolish the post of governor general. Lady Aberdeen reported that he was charming. And they zealously visited institutions and groups of every denomination and level of importance.

As a climax to their visit, Lady Aberdeen planned the biggest, the most expensive and the most theatrical party ever staged in Toronto. She invited 2,500 people to dinner at the Armouries and called the evening "the Victorian Era Ball." She softened the austere ballroom with green carpets, garlands wrapped around the pillars, and soft electric lights. The Aberdeens spent $2,000 on the food alone: soup, meat pies, cold quail and sweets served by a hundred waiters. Toronto was enchanted.

They had already made a substantial impact on the city with their disarming disregard of hostility. Organizations which had resigned from the National Council of Women were returning contritely, and the social establishment had thawed to such an extent that Lady Kirkpatrick herself attended a farewell surprise tea party given by Mrs. John Strachan (described by the guest of honour as "of the very bluest blood in Toronto").

The new city hall at the head of Bay Street was not yet completed, but some sort of an opening ceremony was arranged just so the Earl of Aberdeen could preside. And when the vice regal couple departed for Ottawa, they found that Toronto had filled their railway car with roses.

A lady's toilette was not complete without "delicate and delightful" Crab Apple Blossom perfume, that "one could use for a lifetime and never tire of." In the '90s boudoir, Lavender Salts purified air "most enjoyably, while curing headaches."

Acknowledgements

I want to thank the people I "met" while working on this book, those high-principled, blunt and passionate Victorians. Adelaide Hoodless, Lady Aberdeen and John Kelso appeal most because all three hurled themselves into the most unpopular causes of the day – the abuse of women and children – and none of them had any patience for divisive religion or politics. I'm sorry to have missed knowing "Don" Sheppard, editor of *Saturday Night* in the nineties, and Israel Tarte and Goldwin Smith, who must have been lively company. I would have liked to attend a Sunday service, any of the Sunday services, in Reverend Dickey's Unity Church in Skagway in 1898, and watched Sam Steele handle the mob of mad rafters that spring. But I did meet, through our correspondence, Nellie Edwards of Kamoka, Ontario, when she was in her nineties but still able to recall with fresh delight her Victorian childhood. Ella Frayne told me about Manitoba in the nineties, and Florence Hemstreet trusted me with her copy of *The Swan River Valley*, compiled by Mrs. Charles E. Smith and full of tales of the muddiest wagon trail in the world. To all of them, my gratitude.

June Callwood

Photo: Norman Chamberlin

The Author

June Callwood was born in Chatham, Ontario, and began her career in journalism as a reporter for the Brantford *Expositor*. Since then she has written for many other newspapers and magazines, has worked in social services and in radio and television. She was the founder of the Yorkville Digger House in 1966, a project in aid of young people, and Nellie's in 1974, a hostel for women. She has been an active member of the Canadian Civil Liberties Association. In 1969 she was voted B'nai B'rith Woman of the Year, and in 1974 received the City of Toronto Award of Merit. She is the author of several books, among them *Love, Hate, Fear and Anger* and *The Law (Is Not) For Women*.

Index

The page numbers in italics refer to illustrations and captions

Abbott, John J. C., 54, *57*

Aberdeen, Countess of, 20, 29, 30, 32, *57*, 81, 82, 88, 95, 115-16, *118*, 119-23

Aberdeen, Earl of, 20, 30, 32, *57*, *67*, *118*, 119-23

Advertising, *1, 4, 8, 9, 14, 28, 31, 32, 34, 35, 49, 50, 59*, 69, *69, 70, 71, 75, 76, 77, 78, 92, 93, 107, 110, 111, 114, 115, 123*

Agriculture, 7, 8, 9, 37, 49, 70, *92, 93, 93*, 95-98, *104, 105*

Ahearne, Thomas, 69, 70

Ainsworth, Charlie, *99*

Allan Steamship Company, 70

Amalgamated Street Railwaymen, 40

Amateur Hockey Association, 28

Ames, Herbert Brown, 25, *39*, 44

Anaesthetics, 107-8

Anglicans, 49, 81

Anglin, Margaret, *79*

Annexationism, 38, *48*

Anticosti Island, 14

Architecture, 15-16

Arthur, Julia, *78*, 85-86

At-homes, 19, *22-23*

Atkinson, Joseph E., 86

Atlin, B.C., 29

Automobiles, 7, *10*, 70, 77

Banks, 13, 32, 64

Barnum, P. T., 20

Barrie, Ont., 115

Barry, Robertine, 86

Barrymore, Maurice, 20

Beaudet, Louise, *79*

Beaupré, Edward, *21*

Bell, Alexander Graham, 70, 116

Belleville, Ont., 55, 69

Bell Island, Nfld., 63, 65

Belmont, Man., 32

Benedictson, Margaret, 83

Bengough, J. W., *26, 32*

Berliner, Emile, 69

Bicycles, *2*, 7, 8-9, *9, 10*, 66, 68, 69, 70, 70-77, *71, 72, 73, 74, 75, 76, 77*

Birth control, 88

Blake, Edward, 32

Bloomers, 9, 66, 76

Bond, Robert, 64

Books, 19, 38, *39*, 44, *62, 64*, 86, 88, *88, 116*

Bowell, Mackenzie, 54, *55, 57*, 63-64 121

Boys' Brigade, 20-21

Boy's Own Paper, 45

Breweries, *28, 34, 35*

British Columbia, 13, 29-30, 32, 40, *42*, 64, 93

British North America Act, 55

Brothels, 30, 103

Brown, Ernest, *96*

Bucke, Richard Maurice, 112-13

Cacouna, Que., 18, *18*

Calgary, *29*, 93

Canadian Illustrated News, 121

Canadian Journal of Medicine and Surgery, 43, 116

Canadian Magazine, 54, 69, 86, 88

Canadian Medical Association, 108, 114

Canadian National Exhibition, 32

Canadian Pacific Railway, 7, 14, 31, 49, *53*, 59, 69

Canadian Red Cross Society, 116

Cape Breton Island, 39, 59, *61*, 62, 65

Carmack, George, *102, 103*

Carnegie, Andrew, 14

Cartoons, *13, 22-23, 25, 26, 27, 32, 44, 49, 50, 56, 84, 121*

Cartwright, Richard, *121*

Cascapedia, Que., 32

Chadwick, Cassie, *89*

Charities, 40, 44, 49, *64*

Chicago World Exposition, 51-54, 75, 82, 87, 119

Child labour, 7, 39

Children, *45-47*

Children's Aid Society, 44

Chilcoot trail, *100*, 102, 103

Christian Guardian, 44

Churches, 7, 8-9, 40, 44, 49, 55-56, 75, 76, 103-4, 121

Circuses, 20

Classes, social, 8, 14, 16-19, 25, 43-44

Cody, William F., 20

Coleman, Kathleen Blake, 16, 87

Columbia Records, 69

Conception Bay, Nfld., 63

Conservatives, 25, 26, *26*, 27, 38, *48, 51, 52*, 54-55, *57*, 81, 116

Corruption, *26*, 26-28, *27*, 57

Corsets, 9, 16, 84, 87

Crime, 30, 44

Cruickshank, William, *80*

Cummings, Emily, 86

Cushy, Frank, *99*

Cycling, 9, 75

Dances, 20, *62*, 123

Danielle, Charles Henry, *62*

Davidson, Harley, 77

Dawson, N.W.T., *98, 99, 101*, 102, 103, 115, 116

Decoration, 8, 15, *15*

Delineator, The, 86

Denison, Merrill, 75

Depression, 7, 8, 13, 37-43, *44*

Derick, Carrie, 85

Diamond-Tooth Gertie, *99*

Dickey, Robert McCahon, 103-4

Diseases, 44, *64*, 107-16

  beri-beri, 116

  cholera, 113

  diphtheria, 39, 107, 113, 114, 115, 116

  dysentery, 115

  emphysema, 107

  leprosy, 113

  malaria, 115

  sinusitis, 107

  smallpox, 113

  "summer complaint," 81

  tuberculosis, 39, 113, 114, 116

  typhoid, 8, 103, 113, 114-15

Dixon, George, 28-29

Dominion Coal Company, *61*

Dominion Women's Enfranchisement Association, 84

Dougall, Lily, 86

Dow, William, *34*

Dressler, Marie, 85

Drew, Mrs. John, 20

Drought, 7, 37

Duncan, Sara Jeannette, 86, *87*

Durand, Laura Bradshaw, 86

Eaton, Timothy, 14, 15

Eaton's catalogue, 39, 75

Edgar, James, 27

Edmonton, *10*, 84, *85*, 93

Elections, 25-27

  federal, of 1891, *37*, 38, *48*

  federal, of 1896, 25-26, 27, 55-56

Elliott, Ella, 86

Emard, Bishop, 56

Emigration, 7, 36, 37, 51, 60, 104

Equal Rights Association, 51, *51*, 54

Etiquette, 19, *22*, 76

Exploits River, Nfld., 65

Factory Act (Quebec), 39

Farmers' Institutes, 83, *83*

Farm machinery, 14, 69, *92, 105*

Farrer, Edward, *48*

Fashions, *4, 8, 9, 16, 29, 47*, 66-67, *71*, 76, 84, *85*

Fiction 19, 86, *88*

Fires, *58*, 63, 64

Fisheries, 13, 59-62, *63, 64*, 65, 116

  cod, 60-62

  herring, 62

  lobster, 59-60

  salmon, 60

Fleming, Sandford, 59

Fort Qu'Appelle, N.W.T., 93, *94*

Foster, George, 25

Foster, Mrs. George, 121

France, 59-62

Freight rates, 37

Fulford, George, *107*

Furniture, *15*, 29, 39

Gas, 70

Ghost Dance, 93-94

Gibson, Alexander, 13-14

Gibson, Charles Dana, *4*, 16

Gooderham, George, 14

Gower Street (St. John's), *58*

Graham, Hugh, 14

Gramophones, *6*, 7, *16*, 69

Grand Falls, Nfld., 65

Grave-robbing, 109-12

Greenway, Thomas, 55

Grenfell, Wilfred, *64, 65*, 116

Griffintown (Montreal), 38, 44

Grip, 25, 27, 32, 44, 84

Guatemala, 70

Gzowski, Casimir, *15 118*

Gzowski, Lady, *118*

Halifax, 16, *30*, 59, *117*, 123

Harbour Grace, Nfld., 62

Heating, 16, 29, 69

Hébert, Louis, *34*
Heintzman, Gerhard and Theodor, *16*
Henderson, Robert, *103*
Herchmer, Lawrence W., 37, 94-95
Hilliard, Chris, 98
Hind, E. Cora, 87
Home and School Association, 116
Hoodless, Adelaide Hunter, 81-83, *83*, 85
Hoodless, John, 81
Horses, *10*, 16-18, 44, *117*
Hospitals, 14, *64*, 108-9, *112, 114, 115,*
   116, *117*
Hotels, 16, *18*, 21, 29, 31, *33, 34, 35*, 77
Hours of work, 7, 30, 39, 40, *44*
Houses, 8, *10*, 13, *15*, 18, 104
Humane Society, 44

Immigrants and immigration, 7, 8, 30,
   40, 64, *92*, 93, *93*, 104, *104, 112*, 113
Indians, *42*, 93-95, *94, 95, 97*, 98
Industrial Banner,, 44
Industrial League, 37
Inoculation, 107
Intercolonial Railway, 59
International Council of Women, 121
Inuit, 116
Inventions, 69-70
Irish Canadians, 51
Irving, Henry, 20, 85
Irwin, May, *79*, 86

Jarvis Street (Toronto), 16, 123
Jasper Avenue (Edmonton), *10*
Johnson, Pauline, 20, *20*
Julien, Henri, *56, 121*

Keane, Thomas W., 20
Kellie, "Pot-Hole," 29
Kelso, John, 43-44
Kimberley, B.C., 70
King, William Lyon Mackenzie, 44
Kingston, Ont., *10, 53*
Kirk, Robert, 115
Kirkpatrick, Lady, 19, 123
Klondike, the, 29, 70, 71, 93, 98-103,
   104, 116
Klondike News, The, 102
Knights of Labor, 40

Labatt's, *34*
Labor Advocate, 25, 39, 44
Labour movement, 7, 14, 40, 44, *44*

Labrador, *64, 65*, 116
Laflèche, Louis-François-Richer, 51, 56
Lamore, Nellie, *99*
Lancet, The, 87
Land offices, 104
Langevin, Hector, *26*, 27, *27*
Language question, 7-8 *12*, 49, 51, *51*,
   55-56
Lardeau City, B.C., 29
Laurentide Pulp Mill, Grand'Mère, Que.,
   12
Laurier, Sir Wilfrid, *26*, 27, 32, *52*, 55-56,
   56, 104, *107*, 116, 121, *121*, 123
Leduc, Ozias, *46*
Lee, Erland, 82-83
Lethbridge, N.W.T., 31
Liberals, 25, 26, *26*, 27, 32, 38, *48, 52,*
   55-56, 81, *107*, 116
Lighting, 10, *12*, 29, 69
Liquor, 8, 14, *24*, 25, *25*, 26, 29, *30*,
   30-32, *31, 32*, 94
Little Champlain Street (Quebec), *41*
London, Ont., 21, 26, 40, *42*, 108, 112
Lower, A. R. M., 51
Lower Town (Quebec), *41*
Lumber, 62

McCarthy, D'Alton, 51, *51*, 54, *54*
McCauley, Matt, *85*
McClung, Nellie, 83
McDonald, Big Moose Alex, *99*
Macdonald, John A., 25, *26*, 38, *48,*
   51, *51, 52, 53*, 54, *57*
Macdonald, Lady, 121
Macdonald, William, 14
McDougall, John, 95
McGreevy, Thomas, *26*, 27, *27*
Mackenzie, William, 69
McMaster, Elizabeth, 116
Manitoba, 31-32, 69, 83
Manitoba Equal Suffrage Society, 83-84,
   116
Manitoba schools question, 7-8, 29, 49,
   54, 55-56, *56, 57*
Mann, Donald, 69
Maritime Provinces, 32, 49, 59, *59*
Massey, Hart, 14, 85
Massey, Vincent, 51
Massey Hall (Toronto), 14, 25-26, 83
Massey-Harris Company, 14, 69, 75, 92
Massey's Magazine, 29, *119*
Mather, Margaret, *79*

Mathers, C. W., *96, 97*
Meadows, Arizona Charlie, *99*
Medical training, *107*, 109-12, *116*
Medicine, 7, *14, 64, 107*, 107-116, *109,*
   110, 111, 113, 114, 115
Medicine shows, 20
Mercier, Henri, 14
Mercier, Honoré, 51
Methodists, 30, 44, 51
Métis, 93
Militia, 7, 21, 40, 51
Mining and mineral deposits, 30, 62, 63,
   65, 98
   coal, 39, 59, *61*
   copper, 59
   gold, 7, 29, 70, 93, 98-102, *102*
   iron, 65
   lead, 59
   silver, 29, 70
Minstrel shows, *1*
Miskell, Caroline, *79*
Missionaries, 93, 94, 95
Molson's, *34*
Mollison, Ethel, *79*
Montreal, *11*, 21, 25, *31*, 38, 39, *39*, 40,
   44, 69, 108
Moodie, John, 69, 70, 74, 75
Moravian Brothers, *65*
Morris, Isaac, 60, 63
Motorboats, 69
Mount Stephen, Lord, 14

National Council of Women, 81, 85, 116,
   121-22, 123
Newfoundland, 59-65, *59, 60, 63*, 70
Newspapers, 9, 14, 16, 19, 29, 40, *40*,
   51, *53*, 69, 70, 86-87, 122
   Atlin *Claim,* 29
   Edmonton *Bulletin,* 70
   London *Daily Mail,* 60
   Milton *Reformer,* 27
   Montreal *Gazette,* 40, 51, 109
   Montreal *La Patrie,* 26, 86
   Montreal *Star,* 14, *56*, 86, 121
   New York *Times,* 27
   St. John's *Daily News,* 64
   St. John's *Herald,* 64
   Toronto *Evening News,* 40, 86
   Toronto *Globe,* 27, *48*, 51, 86
   Toronto *Mail,* 16, *52*
   Toronto *Mail and Empire,* 18, 44, 86
   Toronto *World,* 43-44

Washington *Post,* 86
Whitby *Chronicle,* 76
Winnipeg *Free Press,* 86
Nickinson, Charlotte, 85
North West Mounted Police, 30-31, 37,
   93, 94, 98, *98*, 102-3, *121*
North-West Territories, 30-31, 55
Nova Scotia, 49, 59
Nursing, *64, 65, 108*, 109, *114*, 115-16,
   121

Octagon Castle (St. John's), *62*
Office workers, *11, 61*
Oil, 13, 70
O'Neill, James, 20
Ontario Medical Association, 116
Ontario School of Art, *80*
Opium, 30, 113
Orange Order, 21, 51, 54, 123
Oregon Jew, the, *99*
Osler, William, *107*, 109
Ottawa, 51, 121
Ottawa Valley, 40

Painting, *36, 45, 46, 80*
Peace River, N.W.T., 104
Petrolia, Ont., 13
Photography, *17, 96-97*
Pianos, *15, 16*
Place d'Armes (Montreal), *11*
Placentia, Nfld., *62*
Plebiscites, 31, 32
Poker, 29, 30, *99*
Political meetings, 9, 25-26
Port aux Basques, Nfld., 62
Port-au-Port, Nfld., 59
Postal service, *128*
Prairies, 37, 95-98, 104
Presbyterians, 49, 51, 81, 103-4, 120
Prices, 8, 9, 13, *15*, 18, *19*, 38-39, 60, *62*,
   69, 75, 104, 120
Princess Street (Kingston), *10*
Privy Council, Judicial Committee of, 55
Prohibitionism, 8, *24*, 29, *30*, 31, 31-32, 83
Prostitutes, 30, 43, 44, *100*, 103
Protestant Protective Association, 51
Psychiatry, 112
Pulp and paper, *12*, 13, 65

Quebec, 7-8, 32, 49-51, 55-56
Quebec City, 20, *41*, 114, 123
Quebec Harbour Commission, 27

Queen's Plate, 16, 18
Queen Victoria, 7, 54, 81
    Diamond Jubilee, *6*, 7, 21, 87

Racial and religious bigotry, *49*, 49-56,
    50, 121-22
Rag Time Kid, the, *99*
Railways, 13, 14, 29, 31, 69, 93, 95, 104
    Newfoundland, 59, 62-64, *63*, 65, 70
Regina, 120
Reid, George A., *36, 45*
Reid, Robert, 62, 64, 65
Rents, 38-39
Riel, Louis, 7, 49, 93
Riley, James Whitcomb, 20
Ritchie, Grace, *85*
Roberts, Sarah Ellen, 98
Roman Catholics, 49, 51, 54-56, 120,
    121, 123
Rossland, B.C., *33*, 98

St. James Street (Montreal), *11*
St. John's, *58*, 59, 60, 62, *62*, *63*, 64, *64*
Saloons and taverns, 24, 25, 29, 30, *30*,
    31, *34, 35, 64, 99*
Salvation Army, 20-21, *42*
Sandon, B.C., 29
Sao Paulo Light and Power Company,
    69-70
Sarnia, Ont., 13
Saturday Night, 27, 40, *40*, 75, 88   ·
Sault Ste. Marie, Ont., 13
Saunders, Margaret Marshall, 86
Saunders, William, 70
Schools, 9, 39, *64, 81, 94*
Schultz, Mr. and Mrs. J. C., 121
Scientific American, 70
Seal hunt, 60, *60*
Servants, 8, 15, 18, 19, *22*, 88, 120, 123
Sewage disposal, 8, *39*, 44, 69, 114-15
Sexual mores 87-88, *90-91*
Sheppard, Edmund, *40*
Sifton, Clifford, 104, *104*
Simpson, Robert, 14
Simpson-Hayes, Catherine, 86
Sitting Bull, 93
Skagway, 102-3
Slums, 9, *38*, 38-39, *39*, 43, 44, 114
Smith, Goldwin, 38, 81, 123
Social welfare, 9, 44, *64*, 116·
Songs, *7*
Soper, Warren, 69

Sports, 28-29
    bicycle racing, *69*, 74-5, *77*
    boxing, 28-29
    curling, *28*
    fishing, 18
    hockey, 28, *29, 84*
    horse racing, 18
    lacrosse, 28
    rugby football, 28
    tennis, *29, 82*
    tobogganing, 20
Stanley, Lord, 28
Stanley Cup, 28
Stanley Park (Vancouver), 16, *72*
Steamships, 65, 69
Steele, Sam, *98*, 102-3
Stereoscopes, *17*
Stewart, W. Grant, 116
Stoney Creek, Ont., 83, *83*
Stoves, 7, 69
Strachan, Mrs. John, 123
Strathcona, Lord, 14
Streetcars, electric, *2*, 8, *10*, 70, *120*
Streets, 8, *10, 11, 41, 58*, 63
Strikes and lockouts 7, 40
Summer cottages, 18
Supreme Court of Canada, 55
Surgery, 107-9, *115*
Swan, A. S., 88
Swan River, Man., 104

Tadoussac, Que., *18*
Tariff policy, 13, *26, 32, 37*, 37-38, 55, 75
Tarte, Joseph Israel, *26*, 27, *27*, 56
Telephones, 69
Temperance movement, *24*, 29, *30*, 31-32,
    32, 60, 82, 123
Terry, Ellen, 85
Theatre, 9, 20, *30, 78, 79, 82*, 85-86
Thompson, John, 54, *57*, 121
Thompson Lady, 121
Tisdall, C. E., 14
Toronto, *2, 32, 38*, 40, *42*, 43-44, 55-56,
    75, 123
Tramps, *44*
Treble, Lillian Massey, 85
Truro, N.S., 16
Tupper, Charles, 25-26, 55, *57*, 63,
    121, 123
Twain, Mark, 20, 121

Unemployment, 37, 39, 40

Union Church (Skagway), 103-4
United Fruit Company, 70
Universities, *83*, 85
    McGill, 14, *85*, 108, 112
    Manitoba, 85
    Queen's, 85, *107*, 109-12
    Toronto, 85
Vancouver, *10*, 29-30, *34, 72, 73*
Van Horne, William, *12*, 69-70, 120
Victoria, *10, 82*
Victorian Order of Nurses, 115-16, 121
Victor Records, 69
Voice, 44

Wages and salaries, *12*, 13, 14, 15
Wallace, Clarke, 54
Walsh, Archbishop, 56, 121
Ward, the (Toronto), *38*
Water Street (St. John's), *58*, 64, *64*
Wesley, Peter, *95*
West, the, 93-104
Western Federation of Miners, 40
Western Producer, 87
Wheat, 70, 87, 93, 104
White Pass trail, *100*, 102, 103
Whiteway, William Vallance, 63-64
Willison, John, 51
Willson, Henry Beckles, 62, *63*, 64
Willson, Thomas L., 70
Winnipeg, *116*
Winnipeg Medical Association, 116
Women, status of, 7, 9, 32, *32*, 75, 76,
    81-88
    and higher education, *83*, 84-85, *85*,
    116
Women's Christian Temperance Union,
    83, *116*
Women's Institutes, 83
Women's movement, 8, 81-85, *116*
Wood, Joanna E., 86
Woodbine racetrack (Toronto), 18, 75
Working conditions, 39, 40, 44
Workman, Joseph, 112

X-rays, 108

Yeomans, Amelia, 83-84, *116*
Young Women's Christian Association,
    81-82
Yukon Territory, 7, 29, 98-103, *98*, 115

Zangwill, Israel, 19

Picture Credits

Neither rain nor sleet nor threat to strike stayed this postie from his appointed rounds in 1894.

We would like to acknowledge the help and cooperation of the directors and staff of the various public institutions and the private firms and individuals who made available paintings, posters, mementoes, collections and albums as well as photographs and gave us permission to reproduce them. Every effort has been made to identify and credit appropriately the sources of all illustrations used in this book. Any further information will be appreciated and acknowledged in subsequent editions.

The illustrations are listed in the order of their appearance on the page, left to right, top to bottom. Principal sources are credited under these abbreviations:

CCM   Canada Cycle & Motor Company
FFM   Fenelon Falls Museum
MTL   Metropolitan Toronto Library
NPA   Notman Photographic Archives
                   McCord Museum, Montreal
PAA-EBC   Provincial Archives of Alberta
                   Ernest Brown Collection
PAC   Public Archives of Canada

/1 Private Collection /2 Robert Simpson Co. Archives /4 Private Collection /6 Beaverbrook Art Galleries /7 Private Collection /8 Public Archives of Nova Scotia /9 Private Collection, *Saturday Night* /10 Queen's University Archives; PAA-EBC /11 and 12 NPA /13 *Grip* /14 Private Collection /15 NPA /16 National Library of Canada /17 Mrs. Arthur Woodrow; Private Collection /18 Archives Nationales du Québec /19 Private Collection /20 Brantford Historical Society /21 Archives Nationales du Québec /22 and 23 Private Collection /24 Mrs. Charles L. Shields /25 *Grip* /26 PAC-C3580; *Grip*; PAC-PA33469 /28 Glenbow-Alberta Institute; Provincial Archives of Saskatchewan /29 Lawrence Sherk Collection /30 Dalhousie University Archives /31 PAC-C14075 /32 *Grip*; *Saturday Night* /33 Provincial Archives of British Columbia /34 and 35 Lawrence Sherk Collection /36 The National Gallery of Canada /37 PAC /38 United Church of Canada Archives /39 and 40 National Library of Canada /41 NPA /42 PAC-C14099 /43 Archives du Monastère de L'Hôtel Dieu de Québec /44 *Grip* /45 The Winnipeg Art Gallery /46 National Gallery of Canada /47 NPA; Mrs. Charles L. Shields /48 McCord Museum, Montreal /49 *Grip* /50 Private Collection; *Grip*; *Grip* /51 and 52 PAC-PA25698; PAC-C7126 /53 PAC-L3102; Queen's University /54 Private Collection /55 Hastings County Historical Society Archives /56 PAC; Archives du Monastère de L'Hôtel Dieu de Québec /57 PAC-C697, C698, C696, C690 /58 Newfoundland Public Archives /59 MTL /60 Terry Filgate /61 Public Archives of Nova Scotia /62 Newfoundland Public Archives /63 National Library of Canada /64 and 65 Terry Filgate /66 Dalhousie University Archives /67 Alan Suddon /68 CCM /69 and 70 Private collection /71 *Walsh's Magazine*; *Saturday Night* /72 Vancouver Public Library; Vancouver Public Library; PAC-C24322 /73 Vancouver Public Library /74 Private Collection /75 and 76 FFM /77 Private Collection; *Saturday Night* /78 and 79 Private Collection /80 Art Gallery of Ontario /81 Private Collection /82 Peterborough Centennial Museum; Provincial Archives of British Columbia /83 University of Guelph /84 *Grip*; PAA-EBC /85 PAA-EBC; PAC-C68506 /86 Archives, Eaton's of Canada Limited /87 NPA /88 to 91 Private Collection /92 Massey-Ferguson Limited /93 PAC /94 PAC-C37113 /95 Provincial Archives of Alberta, H. Pollard Collection /96 and 97 PAA-EBC /98 Private Collection /99 University of Washington, Photography Collection, Suzzallo Library /100 PAC-C5394, PA13444 /101 Glenbow-Alberta Institute /102 Provincial Archives of Alberta, H. Pollard Collection /103 Private Collection /104 PAC-80096C /105 PAA-EBC /106 Queen's University /107 Pat Rogal /108 NPA /109 *Grip* /110 MTL; Private Collection; MTL; MTL; Private Collection /112 City of Vancouver, Public Archives /113 Private Collection /114 *Grip*; NPA /115 Montreal General Hospital-McGill University Archives; *Grip* /116 Manitoba Archives /117 Private Collection /118 Ontario Archives /119 Province House Library, Halifax, N.S. /120 Ontario Archives /121 PAC-C3398 /122 *Grip* /123 *Grip* /128 PAC-PA12269

1895

Aluminum first produced in Canada at Niagara Falls, Ont.

Frederick Bell-Smith of Toronto commissioned to paint portrait of Queen Victoria.

Territorial Exhibition opens in Regina.

Pauline Johnson publishes *The White Wampum,* her first collection of poetry.

Mackenzie, Yukon, Ungava and Franklin districts formed.

John Moodie of Hamilton, Ont., uses first motorboat in Canada.

Roentgen discovers X-rays.

Lumière brothers patent the motion-picture camera.

1896

Mackenzie Bowell resigns; Charles Tupper becomes prime minister.

Mackenzie and Mann acquire Lake Manitoba Railway charter, start the Canadian Northern Railway.

Gold discovered in the Klondike by George Carmack and two Indians, Skookum Jim and Tagish Charlie.

Winnipeg Victorias defeat Montreal for Stanley Cup.

Gilbert Parker publishes *The Seats of the Mighty*.

Le Soleil established in Quebec.

Wilfrid Laurier leads Liberals to victory in general election.

George Herrick Duggan sails the *Glencairn I* to victory at the Seawanhaka Cup races.

Donald Smith appointed Canadian High Commissioner to Britain.

Quebec boundary extended to Hudson Bay, adding 188,450 square miles to its area.

Niagara Falls hydroelectric plant opens.

Clifford Sifton appointed minister of the interior. Immigration to the Canadian West begins to boom with 16,835 new arrivals.

1897

Responsible government granted to the North-West Territories.

W. H. Drummond publishes his first volume, *The Habitant and Other French Canadian Poems*.

Dr. Henri Casgrain of Quebec becomes first known Canadian to drive motor car – top speed 18 m.p.h.

Canada celebrates Queen Victoria's Diamond Jubilee.

First Canadian ski races and jumping competitions held near Rossland, B.C.

Emile Berliner establishes the Berliner Gramophone Company in Montreal.